POLITICS OUT OF HISTORY

POLITICS OUT OF HISTORY

■ ■ ■ ■

Wendy Brown

PRINCETON UNIVERSITY PRESS

Princeton and Oxford

Library of Congress Cataloging-in-Publication Data

Brown, Wendy.
Politics out of history / Wendy Brown.
p.   cm.
Includes bibliographical references and index.
ISBN 0-691-07084-9 — ISBN 0-691-07085-7 (pbk.)
1. Political science—Philosophy. 2. Political science—History.
3. Liberalism. 4. Progress. 5. Feminist theory. I. Title.
JA71 .B76   2001
320′.01′1—dc21   2001016371

TO JUDY,
FOR HONING COURAGE
AND INTELLIGENCE TO
LOOSEN THE HOLD OF
THE PAST ON THE FUTURE
AND
TO ISAAC, MY HIGH DIVER,
WHO LEARNED SO YOUNG
THE PLEASURES OF
TRIUMPHING
OVER FEAR.

CONTENTS

ACKNOWLEDGMENTS

For their careful readings of one or more chapters, I am indebted to Judith Butler, Tom Dumm, Peter Euben, Gail Hershatter, Robert Meister, Helene Moglen, Gayle Rubin, and Joan W. Scott. William Connolly read the manuscript in its entirety and made superb suggestions for improvement; he is a treasured critic. Earlier versions of these arguments were generously engaged by audiences in a number of venues, but I am especially grateful for the interlocutors who worked with rough versions of this material in five seminar settings: the "Future of Gender" seminar of the Pembroke Center for Research on Women (which caught me moralizing against moralism); the "Feminism and Discourses of Power" Residential Research Group of the University of California Humanities Research Institute (where Anne Norton urged us to think about the shape of history and Saidiya Hartmann offered me new perspectives on the materiality of truth); the "Civilizational Thinking" seminar of the Center for Cultural Studies at the University of California, Santa Cruz (which wrestled heroically with the hermeneutics of reading Benjamin); and my graduate course, "Genealogical Politics," at the University of California, Berkeley, and at the Institut für Philosophie of the Johann Goethe University in Frankfurt (where challenges to my crafting of genealogy as a political orientation were relentless *and* gracious).

For financial support of this project at various stages, I am grateful to the University of California Humanities Research Institute, the UC Santa Cruz Division of Humanities, and the UC Santa Cruz and UC Berkeley Academic Senate Committees on Research. I was fortunate beyond measure to have the research and technical assistance of Catherine Newman, Lon Troyer, and Dean Mathiowetz, each superbly competent and of splendid cheer. Dean Mathiowetz also prepared the index. Finally, I was graced by Alice Falk's artful and meticulous work with my text; she is, in my experience, a copyeditor without peer.

Permission to reprint material published elsewhere has been granted as follows:

"Logics of Power in Marx," *Topoi: A Journal of Philosophy* 15 (1996), for a portion of chapter 4; "Genealogical Politics," in *The Later Foucault*, ed. Jeremy Moss (Sage Books, 1998), for a portion of chapter 5; "Angels and Specters: Benjamin and Derrida on Politics without Progress," in *Vocations of Political Theory*, ed. Jason Frank and John Tambornino (University of Minnesota Press, 2000), revised as chapter 7; "Resisting Left Melancholia," *Boundary 2* 26, no. 3 (fall 1999), and *Without Guarantees: In Honour of Stuart Hall*, ed. Paul Gilroy, Lawrence Grossberg, and Angela McRobbie (Verso, 2000), for a small portion of chapter 7.

POLITICS OUT OF HISTORY

ONE

■ ■ ■ ■

INTRODUCTION
Politics Out of History

What, other than anarchy or free fall, is harbored by the destabilization of constitutive cultural or political narratives? When fundamental premises of an order begin to erode, or simply begin to be exposed as fundamental premises, what reactive political formations emerge—and what anxieties, tensions, or binds do they carry? These studies examine political theoretical practices in an era of profound political disorientation. They are concerned with how we navigate within the tattered narratives of modernity, and especially of liberalism, in our time. Working from the presumption that certain crucial collective stories in modernity have been disturbed or undermined in recent decades, they presume as well that such stories remain those by which we live, even in their broken and less-than-legitimate-or-legitimating form.

I do not argue that the constitutive narratives of modernity are behind us, nor that they have been superseded by other narratives. Rather, in casting certain critical features of modern regimes as troubled yet persistent, I suggest that their troubled condition has significant political implications for contemporary practices of political justice. For example, while many have lost confidence in a historiography bound to a notion of progress or to any other purpose, we have coined no political substitute for progressive understandings of where we have come from and where we are going. Similarly, while both sovereignty and right have suffered severe erosions of their naturalistic epistemological and ontological bases in modernity, we have not replaced them as sources of political agency and sites of justice claims. Personal conviction and political truth have lost their moorings in firm and level epistemological ground, but we have not jettisoned them as sources of political motivation or as sites of collective fealty. So we have ceased to believe in many of the constitutive premises undergirding modern personhood, statehood, and constitutions, yet we continue to operate politically as if these premises still held, and as if the political-cultural narratives based on them were intact. Our attachment to these fundamental modernist precepts—progress, right, sovereignty, free will, moral truth, reason—would seem to resemble the epistemological structure of the fetish as Freud described it: "I know, but still . . ."[1] What happens when the beliefs that bind a political order become fetishes?

From each of the narratives, considered more fully below, that have grown unstable in our time, certain key political signifiers emerge that provide the terms through which the chapters of this book are organized: morality (as the basis for political values and judgments), desire (as potentially emancipatory in its aim), power (as logical in its organization and mechanics), conviction (as the basis for knowledge and political action), and progress (as the basis for political futurity). My purpose with these terms is not simply to counsel their rejection or replacement; rather the aim is to develop a critical understanding of their binding function in a certain political and epistemological story, of how this function has been disrupted as the story itself begins to stutter and fragment, and of what kinds of troubling political formation such a disruption provokes.

However, this undertaking is not only retrospective and critical: these studies also consider what political and intellectual possibilities might be generated from our current predicament. When a disintegrating political or cultural narrative seems irreplaceable, panicked and reactionary clutching is inevitable; when this perceived irreplaceability refers to a narrative or formation actually lost, melancholy sets in. So these analyses seek to attenuate reactionary and melancholic responses by considering possible alternatives to what has been destabilized: I ask how we might conceive and chart power in terms other than logic, develop historical political consciousness in terms other than progress, articulate our political investments without notions of teleology and naturalized desire, and affirm political judgment in terms that depart from moralism and conviction.[2] These speculations do not, of course, result in comprehensive or stable substitutes for their predecessors. Rather, they mark partial and provisional orientations for a different inhabitation of the political world; they limn a different genre of political consciousness and political purpose. And their wellspring is not simply redress of incoherence; rather, they issue from an appreciation of the need for reprieve from a low-lying despair in late modern life, a despair about the very capacity to grasp our condition and craft our future.

Two seemingly opposite effects attend the emancipation of history (and the present) from a progressive narrative and the dispossession of political principles and truths from solid epistemological and onto-logical grounds. On the one hand, there is certain to be a wash of insecurity, anxiety, and hopelessness across a political landscape for- merly kept dry by the floodgates of foundationalism and metaphysics. On the other hand, out of the breakup of this seamless historiography and ground of settled principles, new political and epistemological possibilities emerge. As the past becomes less easily reduced to a single set of meanings and effects, as the present is forced to orient itself amid *so much* history and *so many* histories, history itself emerges as both weightier and less deterministic than ever before. Thus, even as the future may now appear more uncertain, less predictable, and perhaps even less promising than one figured by the terms of modernism, these same features suggest in the present a porousness and uncharted potential that can lead to futures outside the lines of modernist presumptions. This book lives in those paradoxes—simultaneously taking the measure of our anxieties about what we have lost and kindling possibility from what those losses may release us to imagine.

· · · ·

The stories constitutive of modernity are many, complex, and vary significantly by time and place; those that more narrowly undergird the doctrines and practices of liberalism are no tidier. But a few stories crucial to both, generating both the building blocks of the political and its temporality, may be capturable in a few broad brush strokes.

Teleological and Progressive History. The conviction that history has reason, purpose, and direction is fundamental to modernity. This belief has a temporal dimension: modernity itself is imagined to have emerged from a more primitive, religious, caste- and kin-bound, inegalitarian, unemancipated, bloody, unenlightened, and stateless time. And it has a corresponding geographic and demographic dimension: Europe is presumed to be at the heart of this emergence, with other parts of the globe (to various degrees) lagging behind. Modernity is incoherent without both of these dimensions, as is liberalism, the signal political formation that operationalizes each dimension as a foundational political truth.

But modernity is not only premised on the notion of emergence *from* darker times and places, it is also structured *within* by a notion of continual progress. A fundamental Enlightenment precept, the thesis that humanity is making steady, if uneven and ambivalent, progress toward greater freedom, equality, prosperity, rationality, or peace emerged in a variety of explicit formulations in the eighteenth and nineteenth centuries. For Hegel, the world was growing ever more rational; for Kant, more peaceful; for Paine, more true to principles of natural right; for Tocqueville, more egalitarian; for Mill, more free and reasonable; and for Marx, perhaps, all of the above.[3] Today, however, it is a rare thinker, political leader, or ordinary citizen who straightforwardly invokes the premise of progress. In the Euro-Atlantic world, intellectuals of both Right and Left proclaim the "end of history" or an era of "posthistoire." And even as much contemporary political rhetoric in America crows over the benefits of technological advances and the country's growing wealth, it also refers repeatedly to ground lost—economically, morally, and socially—and harks back to a Golden Age in the past. "Family values" talk from all parties conjures an imagined past of happy, moral, and intact families, free from the corruptions of popular culture, libidinal selfishness, illegitimate children, and working mothers. Similarly, welfare state liberals treat growing disparities of wealth in America, and the retreat from half a century's commitments to state amelioration of poverty, as the abandonment of principles once taken as untouchable and as the very signature of progress. Even the iconoclastic left critic Gore Vidal locates the "golden age" of America in the years 1945 to 1950 (approximately the same period invoked by Bob Dole as the last time that America was wrapped in rich moral fabric).[4] In that slim postwar half decade, Vidal argues, intellectual life expanded, the arts flourished, the economy boomed, and the promise of an accomplished and prosperous polity seemed realized. Then came the Korean War, Harry Truman's national security state and its accompanying debt, McCarthyism, and the general unraveling of American promise, an unraveling whose trajectory still traces the course of our lives today.[5]

What makes Vidal's mytho-historical account signal for our time is the figuring of corruption and decline of a once-great polity. That theme, of course, is not new: it framed Thucydides' telling of the Peloponnesian Wars, and Machiavelli's account of the demise of ancient Rome and decline of *quattrocento* republican Florence. But this premodern narrative of history's movement, theorized explicitly as cyclical by Aristotle and Vico, gave way in modernity to a forthrightly *progressive* story, one promising steady improvement in the human condition. Modernity itself is premised on the imagined breaking of medieval fetters on everything from individual happiness to knowledge to freedom to national wealth. For the most part, only modernity's critics (who are also critics of liberalism)—Burke, Rousseau, Nietzsche—have questioned or challenged its forward movement. That intellectuals and politicians are now gazing backward to glimpse better times suggests an important destabilization of the presumption of progress and of the claims and hopes that issue from such a presumption.

It is not only liberal democracies that appear to have lost the thread of progress in history. In postcommunist states, the "triumph of liberalism" heralded by Western pundits in 1989 was short-lived; within eighteen months, intense civil and constitutional conflicts revealed that neither *liberalism* nor *triumph* appropriately named what was unfolding, that there could be no simple resumption of a modernizing narrative temporarily interrupted by fascism, post–World War II Balkanization, and forty-three years of state communism. This collapse of expectations resulted not only from the wars in the former Yugoslavia and in Chechnya, not only from the rise of racism, ethnic conflict, and anti-Semitism across Europe in the wake of 1989. It resulted as well from the obvious impossibility of postcommunist states' participating in the wealth enjoyed by First World nations, from intensely corrupt political formations such as the Mafeeya in Russia, from the devastating consequences for the majority of the population (and especially women) of dismantling the welfare state institutions and employment guarantees of the communist period, and from the limits of "liberalization" or "democratization" in redressing any of these developments.

Like its counterparts felt by politicians and the public at large, contemporary academic doubt about the modernist narrative of progress issues from a variety of points on the political spectrum. While some hold that history's long march has come to an end as liberalism has triumphed around the globe, others argue that this march was always a fiction, and still others insist that something called "postmodernism" heralded the end of progress, totality, and coherence even if history had unfolded progressively up until that point.[6] The tension among these views leads to a question about the nature of the relation between an erosion of the progress narrative in life and in thought. Certainly the relation is not straightforwardly causal, in either direction, but neither is it wholly contingent. Yet it is clear at the very least that recent changes in the character of world history—including all that travels under the rubric of globalization, the emergence of significant nonstate national and international actors, the end of a bipolar international order, and the ambiguous development of identity-based political formations—have catalyzed popular and intellectual historical consciousness. One could also say this: the common instigators of the intellectual and political challenges to progress are certain concrete historical phenomena that include, *inter alia*, the contemporary character of capitalism and the contemporary character of liberalism. Various recent studies in political economy suggest that capitalism in the last quarter of the twentieth century, while displaying certain continuities with earlier forms (e.g., the drive for profit and the ceaseless spawning of new commodities and social effects), nonetheless has taken a qualitatively different turn. Included in the shift from "organized" to "disorganized" capitalism are a national deconcentration of capital and a dispersal rather than concentration of production; a decline in the importance of cartels, unions, and collective bargaining; a growing separation of banks from industry; a decline in the absolute and relative size of the working class (defined as manual workers in manufacturing and extraction); a decline in average plant size; a decline in the importance of individual wealth-holders; and a decline in industrial cities and industry-centered wealth.[7] None of this suggests the diminished dominance of capital; to the contrary, the phenomenon loosely termed "globalization" signifies the ubiquity of capitalist social relations across the globe and the penetration of capital into nearly every crevice of every culture. But the steady geographic and demographic concentrations of wealth, capital, finance, and production that have characterized capitalism for the past two hundred years appear to have given way to more fragmented, dispersed, intricate, transient, and even somewhat ephemeral formations. Thus, Marx's most important condition for the development of the contradiction that would finally break capitalism—relations of production that would "simplify class antagonisms . . . [such that] society as a whole is more and more splitting up into two great hostile camps, into two great classes directly facing each other"[8]—now seems as empirically remote as it is metaphysically alien.

Liberalism has undergone a parallel transformation, from a political order in which the universal rights of man were the unquestioned premise of social justice and social change to one in which both the standing of universalism and the relationship of rights to freedom have been widely challenged. How the disruption of the status of the universal in liberalism undermines the progress narrative is captured in a general questioning (if not outright rejection) of assimilationist and integrationist formulations of social change and the adoption of identity-based justice claims and local nationalisms.[9] Moreover, perceived stratifications and exclusions in liberal orders along lines of race, class, gender, and sexuality not only challenge egalitarian civil and political enfranchisement as the primary criteria of justice; they also expose the formal equality promised by liberalism as severely compromised by the character of a (white, bourgeois, male, heterosexual) hegemonic subject. An understanding of liberal universalism as not simply containing a history of excluded others but as having a specific normative content—heterosexual and patriarchal families, capital, and "property in whiteness"—erodes the credibility of its classic story of progressively widening its scope of freedom and equality, extending the goods of enfranchisement and abstract personhood to more and more of the world's populations. In short, liberalism's sharp encounter in recent decades with its constitutive outside and constitutive others disturbs its universalist premises and promises—and disturbs as well the story of emancipatory and egalitarian progress on which much of liberalism's legitimacy is pinned.

The Emergence of the Sovereign Subject and Rights-Based Freedom. The fiction of the autonomous, willing, reasoning, rights-bearing subject convened by modernity is articulated in liberal democratic constitutions and a host of other liberal institutions. Liberalism presumes sovereign individuals and states, both as units of analysis and as sites of agency. Individuals are cast as sovereign insofar as they devise their own aims and direct and are accountable for their actions. The sovereign state, similarly, is one presumed capable of managing its collective internal affairs and asserting its interests in the external world; these capacities are what justify the state technically and legitimize it politically in an order in which "the people" are said to rule.

Both state and individual sovereignty require fixed boundaries, clearly identifiable interests and identities, and power conceived as generated and directed from within the entity itself. In late modernity, none of these requirements is met easily, given a globalized economic order, unprecedented migrations of peoples across national borders, and relatively new forms of social power that increasingly undermine the notion of the self-made and self-directed individual or state subject. As the global economy grows ever more complex and integrated, both the state and the individual are increasingly frustrated in their sovereign intentions by forces beyond their control and often beyond their comprehension as well.[10] Faced with a plethora of transnational economic actors, forces, and movements, in the late twentieth century the idea of a unified, pursuable national economic interest became largely comic, despite the fact (and vastly complicating the fact) that national economies remain politically and economically significant. And migrations of peoples have reached such proportions that the strenuous legal and political efforts to distinguish, for example, "true Americans" or "native Hawaiians" from alien others can only be read as a symptom of this disintegration of sovereignty, this erosion of inside-outside boundaries around a state or people presumed cohesive, unified, and sovereign.[11]

Sovereignty is especially troubled by ever more intricate yet disseminated forms of social power—what Michel Foucault identified as the proliferation of disciplinary and regulatory discourses in our time. Amid the variety and complexity of speech and institutional practices that not only position but form us, the self-made, autonomously willing, sovereign subject all but vanishes. How is it possible to sustain the conviction that we devise and pursue our own ends when we are so patently the effects of such powers? How, too, does the figure of a unified, coherent, and agentic state appear severely compromised by the distinctive military, counterintelligence, bureaucratic, welfare, and market forces that assault it? How is this figure of the state even undone by the historically unparalleled density and relative autonomy of what is often regarded as *the* state discourse, the law?

Within liberal discourse, the usual alternative to a belief in sovereign subjects is a systems framework in which power is conceived as operating according to certain logics and laws that produce and locate subjects, whether they be states or individuals. There are many versions of this narrative: Marxist, Parsonian, and Habermasian theory, international balance of power theory, psychoanalysis, and so on. However, like the sovereign models, system-based formulations of power, which presume lawlike behaviors and analytic totality, have come under attack on numerous fronts. Foucaultian genealogies, philosophical antifoundationalists, theories of post-Fordist capitalism, and recent challenges to both orthodox international relations theory and psychoanalysis—each contests the fiction of the totality and the axiomatic laws of movement on which both the principles and the particular content of such systems are premised.

When sovereignty is eroded, can the rights rooted in the presupposition of sovereign entities—ranging from subjectivity to statehood—remain intact? What stable, bounded source confers them? What stable, bounded, self-identical subject employs them? What independent, emancipatory force can they continue to claim? From the French Revolution onward, the liberty promised by liberal doctrine has essentially been defined through rights, and the expansion of the quantity and purview of rights is equated with the expansion of freedom. The presumably universal reach of rights in liberal constitutional orders has also implied historically that a quantitative increase in rights generates a quantitative increase in equality. These equations have been disrupted from at least three directions. First, the proliferation of rights in liberal democracies in the second half of the twentieth century has been figured by many, across the political spectrum, as a development less of freedom than of an increasingly administered society—a civil society of bureaucratic agencies and a civic currency of proceduralism and litigiousness. Second, the anti-statist, libertarian Right has, of late, claimed for itself the freedom-as-rights discourse, as have those reacting against what they claim to be special rights or protections afforded to disenfranchised minorities. Both kinds of claims make it extremely difficult for liberals and leftists to argue that rights unequivocally pave the road to enhanced freedom and egalitarianism. Third, liberals have developed an increasing appreciation of an aspect of rights that was formerly considered primarily by Marxist legal scholars: the acontextual formalism of rights means that rights, though universally distributed, often yield *greater* inequalities in societies in which individuals are unequally situated. In some cases they are as likely to entrench existing powers as to redistribute power.[12] Thus, not only the ontological and epistemological basis of rights but also their concrete function in promoting freedom and equality has been significantly challenged in the last quarter century.

. . . .

The troubling of narratives of progress, sovereignty, and freedom and equality secured by rights disturbs the constitutive premises of liberalism from within. But there has also been a disturbance in liberalism's constitutive outside, in the external terms that define and legitimate it. For most of the twentieth century, liberal legitimacy has been secured not only by various elements of social contract discourse but also by differentiation from the imagined opposites to liberalism. It has taken its identity in relation to the naturalized inequalities of feudalism at its historical rear, the intolerable repressions of state communism at its twentieth-century side, and even the utopian dream of a perfected liberal order ahead. In recent decades, however, the remnants of feudal order in the present have shown through more clearly: individual (and hence popular) sovereignty turns out to be a heady conceit; the contemporary state appears less and less autonomous of the market it claimed to set free; and perhaps most important, the ostensible universality of the state and of liberal civic-political culture has been exposed not only as bourgeois but as relentlessly raced, gendered, and sexed—as shot through with stratifying and subject-producing social powers. This exposure makes even liberalism's promise of abstract personhood problematic, insofar as the aim of treating individuals in abstraction from their social attributes appears both ambiguous with regard to the powers constitutive of subordination and impossible to achieve. There is thus a blurring of the radical break that liberalism heralded between itself and feudalism, putatively achieved in the former's abolition of ideologically naturalized stratifications among ideologically naturalized social groups.

Communism's global collapse in the late 1980s eliminated another crucial touchstone for liberalism's identity, literally removing the opposition against which contemporary liberal freedom could be figured. But in a second, more subtle way during the past quarter century, liberalism lost its moorings in anticommunism. Many of the least defensible elements of twentieth-century communist states, leaving aside overt and routinized political repression, have lately made their appearance in ours: overgrown state size, power, and reach; groaning apparatuses of administration intermixed with a labyrinthine legal machinery; expensive and extensive welfare systems that routinely fail their client populations; inefficient and uncontrolled economies; lack of felt sovereign individuality; and chronic urban housing shortages. I do not mean to deny the important differences between market and state economies, nor between one-party rule and constitutional democracies. But the stark *opposition* between communism and liberalism has been attenuated in recent years, an attenuation whose causes are not limited to the recent collapse of communist regimes.

What is the effect on liberalism of these transformations in its historical and global location and historical self-understanding? What happens to liberalism's organizing terms and legitimacy when its boundary terms change—when its constitutive past and future, as well as its constitutive others, lose their definitive difference from liberalism's present and identity? What is (nineteenth-century) liberal justice without a narrative of progress that situates it between an inegalitarian and unemancipated ancien régime and the fulfilled promise of universal personhood and rights-based freedom and equality? What is (twentieth-century) liberal democracy without communism as its dark opposite? What is liberalism out of these histories, indeed out of history as we have known it, which is to say, out of a history marked by the periodicity of this particular past–present–future and by the temporality of progressivism?

This predicament is too recent and our acquaintance with it too new for thoroughgoing answers to such questions. Here, *Politics Out of History* works primarily in a diagnostic vein. If the legitimacy of liberal democracy depends on certain narratives and foundational presuppositions, including progress, rights, and sovereignty, what happens when these narratives and assumptions are challenged, or indeed simply exposed in their legitimating function? What kinds of political cultures are produced by this destabilization of founding narratives and signal terms? What kinds of politics do these narratives produce in their destabilized or broken form? How does their disintegration affect left and liberal political aims, possibilities, sentiments, and discourse? How do we live in these broken narratives, when nothing has taken their place? And how do we conjure an emancipatory future within a liberalism out of history? If the fabric of (universal) justice premised on the (universal) man of the liberal dream is in tatters, on what do we pin our hopes for a more just society? And without the belief in progressive history carrying liberalism toward whatever this reformulated aim might be, what is the engine of historical movement that would realize these hopes?

While vital and vibrant progressive political challenges to current practices of inequality or unfreedom *can* be built on the basis of partial rather than totalizing critiques and political aims, on the basis of provisional and strategic rather than millenarian and teleological political thinking, we currently live in the shadow and sometimes paralyzing disorientation of the historical and metaphysical losses thus far identified. Consequently, despite ubiquitous contemporary critiques and qualms about rights-based justice, most legal theorists and political activists cling to rights advocacy, less engaging with or refuting than simply refusing these challenges to their work. Similarly, most radical and reformist actors remain wedded to progress, even when its credibility is in question, because they imagine all political hope to be invested in a progressive narrative. "Without a notion of progress," my students invariably lament, "what is the point of working for a better world?" As the discussions below of Walter Benjamin, Michel Foucault, and Jacques Derrida will suggest, the equation of progress with political optimism, as well as the equation of a critique of progress with nihilism or despair, may be quite mistaken. Benjamin, in particular, works to sever a redemptive politics from progress, and Derrida's Benjaminian streak moves him to seek political possibility in an order of space and time that is enchanted by spirits other than those of metahistory in general and progress in particular. Indeed, Benjamin and Derrida even suggest that attachment to progress results in a certain political conservatism (an identification with the historical victors who represent progress) and a certain failure to "break" with a current of history that does not contain all political possibility.

But I am getting ahead of my (nonprogressive) story about the condition and possibilities of our political time. Here is a more methodical précis of what follows. In chapter 2, "Moralism as Anti-Politics," I probe one particularly acute symptom of our current predicament: the righteous moralism in so much contemporary political discourse, which I render as a symptom of the political disorientation and political impotence resulting from the troubled narratives identified above. The chapter also examines the anti-intellectualism that political moralism produces, arguing for a mutually vitalizing distinction between political and intellectual life. It is in this spirit of shamelessness about intellectual inquiry shaped by political concerns but unmoored from an obligation to specific political entailments that the remainder of the book proceeds. Chapter 3, "The Desire to Be Punished," considers, through a reading of Freud's theory of masochism, the problem of political desires in subjects whose identity is rooted in social injury, and who can no longer count on the magic of progress to redeem that injury. It queries how the desire for freedom, equality, and political participation can be shaped in subjects who are not only produced through subordination, suffering, and exclusion but are also politically identified with that production and, absent a faith in progress, cannot imagine release from that identity. Chapter 4, "Power without Logic without Marx," considers the problem of conceiving social and political power in terms other than sovereignty or systems. Through a close reading of selected works by Marx, this chapter asks what happens when the logics of scientism, dialectics, and laws of history are shed from Marx's theorization of power, as it considers how power in a postfoundational materialist modality might be conceived without reliance on those logics. It also explores how a reconceptualization of temporal logics (in the form of a critique of progress) inevitably entails a reconceptualization of spatial ones (in the form of a critique of logical entailment and causality). This link is evident in Foucault's overt effort to think about power in spatial rather than temporal terms, an effort that results in a focus on power in disciplinary and regulatory modalities; but it can be seen as well in the intertwining of spatial and temporal logics of power in Marx himself.

Chapter 5, "Politics without Banisters: Genealogical Politics in Nietzsche and Foucault," makes use of the two philosophers to develop a genealogical alternative to progressive and teleological historiography as it is now embedded in contemporary democratic politics. Genealogy is treated not merely as a method of historical inquiry and political analysis, but as an intellectual orientation potentially generative of new political directions. Chapter 6, "Democracy against Itself," begins by examining the fraught relation between theory and democracy and then revisits Nietzsche's thought to consider the possibility of deploying his severe critique of democracy, and of politics generally, to enrich democratic practices. In considering what the singular relationship between critical theory and a democratic political form might be, this chapter speculates about strategies for working against the moralizing and anti-intellectual tendencies in contemporary democracies that are identified in the second chapter. Chapter 7, "Specters and Angels," attempts to craft a fruitful form of historical-political consciousness from the post-Marxist critiques of progress advanced by Walter Benjamin and Jacques Derrida. It centers on the problem of conceiving futurity at "the end of history," that is, in the wake of a progressive understanding of modernity.

None of these studies offers a full-fledged replacement for the waning terms and narratives of modernity. Rather, each examines a few strands of the condition that this waning has produced, attempting to open thought and discern possibility where anxiety, paralysis, and reaction too often dwell. Each avows the mourning as well as the confusion that conditions our work as we attempt to mine potential from the losses of our time. Neither purely despairing nor purely hopeful, each study bears the mixture of heaviness and hope carried in a history that, in the wake of metaphysics and metanarratives, may finally become our own.

T W O

■　■　■　■

SYMPTOMS

Moralism as Anti-Politics

The Left has traditionally distinguished itself from liberal reformers by its object of critique as well as by the drama and scope of its political vision. Rather than attend to what it regarded as contingent injustices in the social order, it criticized more fundamental dynamics of injustice or domination as inherent to the regime. While reformers addressed particular inequities or cruelties within the fabric of capitalism or liberalism, the Left located sources of suffering in what it conceived as the constitutive premises and hence the totality of these arrangements. And it called for the replacement of this totality with a radically more humane and egalitarian order of economic life, to which would correspond a less individualistic, alienated, and socially irresponsible organization of political life.

What becomes of such distinctions when the traditional objects of left critique—liberalism, capitalism, and the state—emerge as the apparently ubiquitous institutions of the present and future? What happens when these objects no longer seem eligible for replacement by alternative economic and political forms but assume only a variety of cultural and historical shapes around the globe? What becomes of the desires animating left critique and fueling left political projects when not only the historical ground but also the political and philosophical foundations of that critique and that project have been compromised beyond recognition?

This condition, in which promising alternatives to liberalism and capitalism have largely vanished, has not emerged only since the fall of the Berlin Wall and disintegration of the Soviet Union. It has been unfolding for almost half a century. Periodically accented by events such as Khrushchev's 1956 speech detailing what the world's unconscious already knew about Stalin's atrocities and similar revelations twenty years later about the nightmare of China's "cultural revolution," the period has been marked as well by various failed Third World experiments in socialist autonomy and by the history of an economically impoverished, as well as culturally and politically repressed Eastern Europe. This history was consummated in the 1980s by the virtual disappearance of the Left in the United States, the strikingly nonsocialist reign of François Mitterand in France, the dramatic shrinking of Communist Parties in Western Europe, and, finally, the crumbling of the Soviet bloc. The Reagan-Thatcher decade, characterized by Stuart Hall as one in which the Left utterly lost its way (while the Right forged a new hegemony out of "the remaking of common sense"), is probably best explained as part of a longer history of the unraveling of the Left: Marxism proved unable to address critical issues of need, desire, and identity formation in late modernity, and Marxist projects failed by almost all economic, political, and eudaemonistic measures.[1] In short, in the second half of the twentieth century, liberalism and capitalism have been quietly consolidating their gains less because they were intrinsically successful than because their alternatives collapsed. Now both appear fat and happy, indeed triumphant, even as they are not always able, in Herbert Marcuse's words of thirty years ago, "to deliver the goods"[2] either by providing stable, just, pluralistic orders or by alleviating poverty, economic deracination, a vacuum in social and political meaning, and the largely unsatisfying work done by those in almost every economic stratum.

If the viability of democratic alternatives to liberal democracy and the metaphysical grounds of the standard left critiques of liberalism both eroded significantly in the last quarter of the twentieth century, from where might the Left draw its inspiration and its instruments of critique? And if those drawn to a left weltanschauung have traditionally found compelling its claims to apprehend a social totality and meaning in history, as well as its promise of a redemptive future, where does this desire live now and, markedly unfulfilled, what form of social expression might it take?

We are well schooled in one answer to this question. What today travels under the name of cultural politics, identity politics, the politics of cultural diversity, new social movement politics, or the politics of new social antagonisms is widely considered to have taken over the ground formerly occupied by a socialist Left. Where there was once the Movement, there are now multiple sites and modalities of emancipatory struggle and egalitarian protest. Similarly, where there was once a millenarian, redemptive, or utopian project around which to organize the various strategies of the political present, such projects have splintered politically at the same time that they have been quite thoroughly discredited by cultural and philosophical critique. Yet this description of a shift in political formations, political analysis, and correlative theoretical articulations does not address the fate of the *desire* for total critique and total transformation, the impulse to wholly indict the structures of the present and stake all on the absolute justice of a radically transformed future. What shape does this desire take when diffused into local, issue-oriented, or identity-based struggles that generally lack a strong alternative vision? In the work of contemporary political activists and thinkers, what has replaced the passionate attachment to a dream of another political, social, and economic world? What are the psychic consequences for political life when total critique is abandoned and the aspirations for total transformation are shattered?[3]

In formulating these questions in terms of the fates of a left sensibility and project, I do not mean to obscure the extent to which they grip some liberals as well. Notwithstanding liberalism's sustained hegemony in the West, key premises underpinning the legitimacy and optimism of the liberal project have been shaken profoundly in recent decades. Liberal universalist and progressive principles have been challenged by the anti-assimilationist claims of many current formations of politicized "differences," including those marked by ethnicity, sexuality, gender, and race; by a political ethos promulgating *agonistic* social relations associated with these cultural differences, as opposed to a model of pluralistic conflicting interests on the one hand, or of general social harmony on the other; and by the patently mythical nature of a progressive political worldview that presumes steady improvement in the general wealth, felicity, egalitarianism, and peacefulness of liberal societies. Undermined by historical as well as intellectual events in the late twentieth century, the seamlessly egalitarian social whole constituting liberalism's vision of the future now appears problematic both theoretically and practically.

Just as leftists are not free of attachment to total critique and total transformation, so liberals are not free of attachment to ontological and political universalism and hence to assimilationist politics. Neither leftists nor liberals are free of the idea of progress in history. Neither can conceive freedom or equality without rights, sovereignty, and the state, and hence without the figures of a sovereign subject and a neutral state. The consequence of living these attachments as ungrievable losses—ungrievable because they are not fully avowed as attachments and hence are unable to be claimed as losses—is theoretical as well as political impotence and rage, which is often expressed as a reproachful political moralism. Put differently, the righteous moralism that so many have registered as the characteristic political discourse of our time—as the tiresome tonality and uninspiring spirit of Right, Center, and Left—can be understood as a *symptom* of a certain kind of loss. Yet insofar as politics is a nonorganic domain in which symptoms transmogrify into forms of action and thence into political formations—nothing is ever *merely* a symptom—this phenomenon also must be understood as constituting a pervasive political and intellectual way of life in contemporary North America.

When genealogy replaces totalizing and dialectical history and contests for hegemony replace progressivist formulations of change, when the future thus becomes relatively continuous with the present, so that radical political discontent can no longer make a home in an analysis of a powerfully determining history and a transformed future, where does it then live? What form does this radical discontent take within the emotional substructure of political expressions and political formations? If, as Nietzsche recognized, impotent rage inevitably yields a moralizing (re)action, how might we succeed in rereading contemporary political life through this recognition? Might it help us understand, for example, the contemporary tendency to personify oppression in the figure of individuals and to reify it in particular acts and utterances, the tendency to render individuals and acts intensely culpable—indeed prosecutable—for history and for social relations? Might it help us understand the paradoxical tendency toward a politics of hypersovereignty and literalism within an ostensibly postsovereign and postliteral theoretical regime—that is, in a discursive epoch when both sovereignty and literalism have been called into question because of the models of the subject, power, and language that they embody? An inquiry along these lines also permits questions about the relationship of moralizing discourse to democratic political possibility and to the kind of free-ranging intellectual inquiry required for the nourishment of a democratic polity. What does the pervasiveness of moralizing discourse *do* to political life, to intellectual life, and, most important, to their complex claims on—and needs for—each other? Why has moralizing discourse become particularly intense in left activist and academic life, and what makes "cultural politics" particularly susceptible to this discourse ultimately subversive of the putatively emancipatory aims of such politics?

· · · ·

Although both morality and moralism take their bearings from and constitute their identity by distancing themselves from what they take to be power, and therefore both lodge uneasily in political life, morality and moralism are not equivalents. Thus, we might begin by distinguishing the problem I am calling political moralism from the older, more familiar problem of morality in politics. Such a distinction is not meant to suggest that morality's place in politics was ever unproblematic, that morality does not persistently risk devolving into moralism, or that morality is a straightforward political good while moralism is a political evil. But I have written elsewhere against moral truths as a substitute for political struggle, relying mainly on adaptations of Nietzsche's genealogical study of (Judeo-Christian) morality; and I now want to rethink an aspect of my critique, and Nietzsche's too, by paying closer attention to the difference between a galvanizing moral vision and a reproachful moralizing sensibility. Previously I argued that certain contemporary moral claims in politics issue from a combination of attachments—both to Truth (as opposed to power) in a postfoundational era and to identity as injury in a political domain of competing survivor stories.[4] Here, I reconsider moralizing politics as marking a crisis in political teleology. I propose to read such politics not only as a sign of stubborn clinging to a certain equation of truth with powerlessness, or as the acting out of an injured will, but as a symptom of a broken historical narrative to which we have not yet forged alternatives.

The *Oxford English Dictionary* offers an unremarkable set of definitions for *morality*: "ethical wisdom; knowledge of moral science . . . moral qualities or endowments . . . moral discourse or instruction . . . doctrine or system concerned with conduct or duty . . moral conduct." However, the same dictionary defines *moralism* as "addiction to moralizing . . . religion consisting of or reduced to merely moral practice; morality not spiritualized." Indeed, one citation suggests that *moralistic* is the opposite of *moral*, as the nineteenth-century theologian Boyd Carpenter discriminates between the two: "Such an action is moralistic rather than moral for it has not been prompted by the sentiment of goodness."[5]

From this account, moralism would appear to be a kind of temporal trace, a remnant of a discourse whose heritage and legitimacy it claims while in fact inverting that discourse's sense and sensibility. At the extreme, moralism may be seen as a kind of posture or pose taken up in the ruins of morality by its faithful adherents; it is thus at once a "fall" from morality, a "reversal" of morality, and an impoverished substitute for, or reaction to, the evisceration of a sustaining moral vision. As an "addiction," the compulsive quality of moralism stands opposed to measured, difficult, and deliberate action that implicates rather than simply enacts the self; as "religion reduced to merely moral practice," it consists of precepts and remonstrances whose spiritual incitation and inflection is lost to history, and whose secular enactment becomes ritualistic—and, not incidentally, often punitive. The element of punishment arises because moralism appears to be, in the Nietzschean sense, a reaction (or, more precisely, a compulsive reproach) to a certain kind of action or power and thus a recrimination against the life force that action or power represents. To continue briefly in a Nietzschean vein, moralism, considered as an effect or consequence of weakened life forces, strikes at what appears to subordinate or humiliate it (but which has actually produced it): expressions of life forces or power. As a codification of disappointment or disenthrallment, it seeks to make a world in its own self-image and thus reproves everything tainted with power. In this way, a strange breed of nihilism—opposition to life itself—disguises itself in the clothing of its opposite: righteous political principle.

But while the distinction between moralism and morality is rendered sharply in dictionaries, in politics the two have a closer relationship. There is, of course, a long tradition of inquiry into the place of morality in politics. In the West, it could be said to extend from Thucydides, the Sophists, and Aristotle's critique of Plato through Machiavelli, Kant, Croce, E. H. Carr, Hans Morgenthau, Martin Luther King, Jr., and Gandhi. These last four names remind us that in the twentieth century, the question of morality's place in politics has mostly been cast as setting "realpolitik" against "moral or religious principle," although this formulation is not, as Machiavelli made clear in his relentless exposé of the Papacy as both an instrument and culture of power, without a certain analytic duplicity. Even in its least philosophical modality, the problematic of morality in politics is usually thought to center on the complex relation between principle and power, or on the important intervals between aim, strategy, action, and effect. Conventional inquiries into morality and politics almost always assume the relationship between principle and power to be fully antagonistic, whether through the notion that "power corrupts" or through its mirror, that "principle is averse to power"; in either case the potential for absolute goodness is conferred on principle and absolute evil on power. It is this assumption that Machiavelli most boldly and Nietzsche most ingeniously reversed. Refusing principle's ruse of representing its aim as indifferent to power—and thereby exposing the will to power in principle and especially, for Machiavelli, in Christian principle—both thinkers sought to depict the power that could play under the name of moral principle disguising itself as unarmed.[6]

Notwithstanding this critique and its more recent embellishments by Foucault, a formulation of the relationship of politics and morality that reduces to "power versus principle" has persisted into the present, especially when violence is at issue. Consider the kind of conundrums generally posed to students contemplating the place of morality in politics: According to what criteria can economic sanctions said to be more humane than other forms of international aggression? Is nuclear warfare uniquely immoral in the history of humankind? Is property damage in the course of civil disobedience consistent with principles of nonviolent protest? When is war as such justified; when is pacifism or nonintervention immoral? Do women have the moral right to determine the fate of fetal life carried in their own bodies? Do humans have the moral right to kill animals? What is common, and commonly irritating, about these questions is that they formulate a moral problem abstracted from the specific context in which such questions arise, and disavow as well the discursive framing through which they are proffered. Precisely for this reason morality often has been regarded by critical political thinkers as not simply a naive but a depoliticizing form of political discourse: consider how different the "moral" question of abortion appears when emphasis is placed on women's near-total responsibility for children in a historically produced context of relative lack of control over the terms of sexual, economic, and political life—that is, in a context of the powers that make and organize gender.

Yet the play of morality in politics is not entirely confined to relatively abstract dilemmas about right action or moral limits to the exercise of power. Whole political formations have taken their bearings from their moral opposition to a historically specific "immoral" regime. The founding and sustaining principle of the Civil Rights movement in the United States was the immorality of racial segregation in a liberal democratic nation; substantively and tactically, the movement staked everything on opposing the differential treatment of citizens in an ostensibly egalitarian order as a moral wrong. It explicitly posed—as did Gandhi's campaigns against British colonial rule and the Indian caste system—moral right *against* power. But these movements also turned principle into an explicit and self-conscious form of power that worked by distinguishing itself in style, bearing, and tactics from the power and interests of the regime it decried.

To be sure, a theological pathos is operative when a rhetorical opposition is established between the virtuous position of the disenfranchised and the iniquity of dominance. This is the pathos Nietzsche denounced as slave morality for its general objection to power as such. But here, Nietzsche may have failed to distinguish adequately between active moral struggles against subordination and the reproaches and nay-saying of what he called slave morality. Certainly, the movements led by King and Gandhi would seem to be instances of the former insofar as they affirmed the capacity of the subjugated to *overcome* their injury, their socially structured subordination, and to assume a place in the world rather than—as Nietzsche insisted slave morality always does—to distribute their suffering in the world, "to make others suffer as the sufferer does."[7]

The shared features of these affirmative moral struggles also distinguish them from projects animated by political moralism: their relatively open, democratic character; their tendency not to vest the evil they are fighting in persons or even in social positions but rather in social arrangements and institutions; and the relative abstractness of their motivating principle—its lack of cultural specificity or attachment to a particular people. While these movements did not wholly eschew the phenomenon of identity produced through oppression, neither did they build solidarity on the basis of that production; rather, solidarity was rooted in shared beliefs. They did not make a cultural or political fetish out of subordinated identities, out of the *effects* of subordination. Moreover, these movements were fueled by opposition to specifically articulated political systems or social arrangements— segregation, colonialism, or caste society—rather than by opprobrium toward persons (whites or the British) or by amorphous campaigns against racism. In a word, these were movements that took shape within the humanist tradition of universal principles, particularly the principles of universal human value and universal human rights.

But if these movements differed markedly from what today often travels under the sign of cultural politics, especially insofar as they eschewed cultivation of identity-bound difference claims, they might be critically interrogated precisely for their unreflexive traffic with humanism—their embrace of universal and even essentialized personhood, their inattention to cultural difference, their relative neglect of the historically contingent and contextual character of political life. Here one would ask both when a movement for inclusion is problematically assimilationist, because indifferent to the norms regulating that assimilation, and also when a movement animated by moral principle can be fouled by the contextually specific political constraints and content with which it must deal. To the extent that the classical invocation of morality in politics entails subscription to universalism, it is not only contemporary antihumanist or posthumanist critics but also those in the "realist" tradition of Machiavelli and Morgenthau who are dubious about the fit between such universals and the contingencies of politics. Indeed, Machiavelli's sharpest criticism of a moral politics pertained not to its naiveté about human motives or human nature but to naiveté about the dynamics of power and fluidity of context in which actions motivated by the finest of intentions produce effects of incalculable tragedy and suffering. Hence Machiavelli's disturbing rumination: "If a prince has [only virtues] and always practices them, they are harmful; and if he appears to have them, they are useful."[8] Because the realm of politics cannot be ordered by will and intention, but is a complex domain of unintended consequences that follow the unpredictable collisions of human, historical, and natural forces, a politics of abstract principle risks missing its aim and indeed producing the opposite of the wished-for result. "Therefore, [a prince] must have a mind ready to turn in any direction as Fortune's winds and the variability of affairs require[;] . . . he holds to what is right when he can but knows how to do wrong when he must."[9] And it may be precisely when the limitations of a politics of morality reveal itself to highly invested players that a moral politics inevitably begins to acquire some of the trappings of a moralizing one. Those who are no longer able to *act* in good-faith accord with their moral vision strike out angrily against the world that affords their adherence only mockery. Life-affirming moral passion in this way converts to life-negating moralizing rancor, an effect that Nietzsche memorably characterized: "this *instinct for freedom* forcibly made latent . . . pushed back and repressed, incarcerated within and finally able to discharge and vent itself only on itself; that, and that alone, is what the *bad conscience* is in its beginnings."[10]

· · · ·

Neither a pure politics of morality nor of realpolitik describes the political or theoretical register in which we are primarily ensconced today. With the exception of a relatively marginal order of religious activists, cultural feminists, and nonviolent peace workers, most leftists and liberals do not subscribe to the opposition between Truth and Power on which both a politics of morality and a politics of realism depend. The conventional (Platonic, Christian, Marxist, and liberal) equation of truth and goodness on one side and power and oppression on the other has been disrupted both by the late modern decentering, multiplication, and politicization of Truth and by critiques of modernist formulations of power as repressive, commodity-like in form, or independent of hegemonic truth claims. Even where these critiques are either unacknowledged or explicitly rejected—where the morality- and truth-bearing capacities of powerlessness are fiercely reasserted against all that has discredited the partnership—the attempt of powerlessness to claim truth is shaken by the crumbling of utopian or millennial political visions: with little hope and no precise architecture for a radically different order, the martyred in *this* world have a sharply attenuated moral-epistemological status. While martyrdom may retain an element of rhetorical force, it is moralistic rather than moral insofar as it no longer can draw on any larger cosmology.[11]

But the loss of conventional epistemological ground for a strong moral position, and even for morality as such, does not quash the moral impulse itself. Here we return along a different path to the question with which we began: what form does this impulse take when it has lost its lodging in an abstract principle and vision of the good . . . when moral claims reduce to moralizing complaint? It is when the telos of the good vanishes but the yearning for it remains that morality appears to devolve into moralism in politics. It is at this point that one finds moralizers standing against much but for very little, adopting a voice of moral judgment in the absence of a full-fledged moral apparatus and vision. Alternatively, the moralizer refuses the loss of the teleological and becomes reactionary: clinging without logical ground to the last comforting frame in the unraveling narrative—pluralism, the working class, universal values, the Movement, standpoint epistemology, a melting pot America, woman's essential nature—whatever it was that secured the status of the true, the status of the good, and their unbroken relationship. This, too, is a form of moralizing, but it takes the especially peculiar shape of reproaching history by personifying and reifying its effects in particular individuals, social formations, theories, or belief structures. Thus, for example, some leftists have recently called for the resuscitation of universal political identity and a universal progressive political aim, while blaming something they name "postmodernism" or "identity politics" for the loss of these goods and for the promulgation of highly fractured (and fractious) political claims and aims. In a similar vein, many denounce as morally or politically bankrupt those theoretical formations that call into question the privileged ontological and epistemological status of the oppressed or that do not prescribe the nature of the good. "If poststructuralist theory cannot tell us what to value and what to fight for," a colleague of mine recently queried a graduate student in a qualifying examination, "what can possibly be its worth for political thinking?" But dubiously grounded political *doctrine*, rather than political thinking, would seem to be what my Marxist colleague was really mourning. And democratically contestable, partial, provisional political judgments appeared to be what he was moralizing against.

Despite its righteous insistence on knowing what is True, Valuable, or Important, moralism as a hegemonic form of political expression, a dominant political sensibility, actually marks both analytic impotence and political aimlessness—a misrecognition of the political logics now organizing the world, a concomitant failure to discern any direction for action, and the loss of a clear object of political desire.[12] In particular, the moralizing injunction to act, the contemporary academic formulation of political action as an imperative, might be read as a symptom of political paralysis in the face of radical political disorientation and as a kind of hysterical mask for the despair that attends such paralysis. This is the very dynamic Nietzsche denoted as issuing from the "instinct for freedom forcibly made latent." However tendentious the language of instinct, what remains compelling in Nietzsche's understanding of the dynamic in which a desire for freedom or the will to power is turned back on itself is the idea that a life force flattened into a passive or paralyzed stance toward the world turns against life as it turns against itself; it turns against that which incites the subject to overcome itself. Indeed, paralysis of this sort leads to far more than an experience of mere frustration: it paradoxically evinces precisely the nihilism, the antilife bearing, that it moralizes against in its nemesis—whether that nemesis is called conservatism, the forces of reaction, racism, postmodernism, or theory.

While moralizing discourse symptomizes impotence and aimlessness with regard to making a future, it also marks a peculiar relationship to history, one that holds history responsible, even morally culpable, at the same time as it evinces a disbelief in history as a teleological force. When belief in the continuity and forward movement of historical forces is shaken, even as those forces appear so powerful as to be very nearly determining, the passionate political will is frustrated in all attempts to gain satisfaction at history's threshold: it can acquire neither an account of the present nor any future there. The perverse triple consequence is a kind of moralizing *against* history in the form of condemning particular events or utterances, personifying history in individuals, and disavowing history as a productive or transformative force. This triple effect, and the limits it imposes on a substantive emancipatory politics, is captured in the often overburdened significance ascribed to "subject position"—one's own and others'—in our time. Having lost our faith in history, we reify and prosecute its *effects* in one another, even as we reduce our own complexity and agency to those misnamed effects.

. . . .

Morality stands in an uneasy relationship to the political insofar as it is always mistrustful of power; and it bears a slightly truncated relationship to the intellectual insofar as it is rarely willing to explore the seamy underside of righteousness or goodness in politics. Moralism is much less ambivalent: it tends to be intensely antagonistic toward a richly agonistic political or intellectual life. Moralism so loathes overt manifestations of power—its ontological and epistemological premises are so endangered by signs of action and agency—that the moralist inevitably feels antipathy toward politics as a domain of open contestation for power and hegemony. But the identity of the moralist is also staked against intellectual questioning that might dismantle the foundations of its own premises; its survival is imperiled by the very practice of open-ended intellectual inquiry. It is thus in a moralistic mode that the most expansive revolutionary doctrines—liberalism, Maoism, or multiculturalism—so often transmogrify into their opposite, into brittle, defensive, and finally conservative institutions and practices. Here I offer an example from within the academy.⌉

At a workshop on the present and future of "cultural studies"— where this amorphous academic entity was taken to include women's studies, sexuality (queer) studies, ethnic studies, and certain types of American and other area studies—I reflected aloud on worries I have been harboring for some time about the institutionalization of political identities as academic programs. My focus was women's studies, which I know best, and the first part of my presentation went as follows:

> I have had a number of conversations in the last few years that may bear kinship with some that American Communist Party members had with each other in the fifties. Here is the prototype: I meet someone whose name has long been familiar to me as both a feminist scholar and trenchworker in the field of women's studies. She helped build women's studies at her institution and for years has defended it against onslaughts—political, financial, and internal—threatening its survival. She is possibly on the editorial board of one or more feminist journals, and is prominent in various feminist professional and political associations. She bears the scars and the pride of years of feminist work, both inside and outside the academy.
>
> Because we have not met before but, like members of the Old Left, we have fundamental work and commitments in common, we begin getting to know each other by talking about that work. And then— the shift is always imperceptible—we begin to connect through another bond, a complexly traitorous bond, as it becomes evident that we are both taking distance from women's studies. We may chair programs in it, publicly defend it, teach courses in it, have part or all of our faculty appointment in it, and know that it not only once gave us life but perhaps now butters our bread. But we don't identify with it anymore, or we don't need it anymore, or our work isn't located there anymore, or perhaps most devastating of all, we don't believe in it anymore.
>
> Why are these conversations happening and how might they usefully go public? Why are certain established feminist scholars having

such sentiments, and why are younger scholars notably not drawn to women's studies? What has it meant to institutionalize a program rooted in contingent social identity, how has our own scholarship imploded this identity and exposed the many facets of its contingency, and what is the consequently fraught or conservative nature of the intellectual position women's studies now finds itself having to occupy in order to persist?

Here is a second way into this problem. The women's studies program at my university recently undertook that frightening project of self-scrutiny known as curriculum revision. What brought us to this point is itself interesting. For a number of years, we limped along with a set of requirements consisting of an odd mix of the generic and the political. *The generic*: students were required to take a three-term sequence consisting of "Introduction to Feminism," "Feminist Theory," and "Methodological Perspectives in Feminism," a sequence marked by distinctions scandalously at odds with the expansive understanding of theory and the critique of methodism putatively fundamental to feminist inquiry. *The political*: the only other content-specific requirement for the major was a course called "Women of Color in the United States." This strange combination of genres in the curricular requirements underscored for students the isolated intellectual (and putatively nonracialized) character of something called theory, the isolated (and putatively nontheoretical) political mandate of race, and the illusion that there was something called method (applied theory?) that unified all feminist research and thinking. It also meant that most women's studies students regarded the requirements as something to be borne, and the major as having its rewards elsewhere. Finally, and most disturbing, the limited and incoherent nature of these requirements as a course of study meant that some of our students were obtaining BAs on the basis of very poor educations, something women have had too much of for too long.

But what happened when we finally sat down to revise the curriculum is even more interesting than what the previous curriculum symptomized. We found ourselves absolutely stumped over the question of what a women's studies curriculum should contain. Since, in addition to trying to provide curricular integrity, we were also trying to address faculty frustration about students not being well enough trained in anything to ever provide rewarding classroom exchange in the faculty's areas of expertise, we focused intently on the question of what would constitute an intellectually rigorous program as well as an intellectually coherent one. We speculatively explored a number of different possibilities—a thematically organized curriculum, pathways that roughly followed the disciplines—but each possibility collapsed under close analysis. We also found ourselves repeatedly mired in a strange chasm between faculty and students in the program: Most of our 200-plus majors were interested in some variant of feminist sociological or psychological analysis—experientially, empirically, and practically oriented. Not one of our core faculty worked in sociology, psychology, or ahistorical empirical studies.

If the practical project we set for ourselves was running aground, certainly we were in the grip of an important historical-political problem. Why, when we looked closely at this thing so hard fought for and now academically institutionalized, could we find no there there? We were up against more than the oft-discussed divide between women's studies and feminist theory, the political insidiousness of the institutional division between ethnic studies and women's studies, a similarly disturbing division between queer theory and feminist work, or the way that the ostensibly less identitarian rubric of cultural studies promises to relieve these troubling distinctions. And we were up against more than the paradox that the disciplines which have been so denatured in recent years are also apparently that which we cannot do without, if only to position ourselves against them within them. We were also up against more than the dramatic fracturing of women's studies as a domain of inquiry during the 1980s—the fact that contemporary feminist scholarship is not in mass group conversation but is, rather, engaged with respective disciplines, or bodies of theory, that are themselves infrequently engaged with each other. And we were up against more than the ways that this decade's theoretical challenges to the stability of the category of gender, and political challenges to a discourse of gender apart from race, class, and other severe markers of identity, constituted very nearly overwhelming challenges to women's studies as a coherent endeavor. We were up against more than the fact that the impulses which had fomented women's studies have now disseminated themselves—appropriately, productively, and in ways that profoundly challenged the turf women's studies had claimed as its own.

We were up against more than any one of these challenges because we were up against all of them. But rather than considering them in their specificity, I want to suggest that together, they call us to account for our effort to *institutionalize* as curriculum, method, field, major, or bachelor of arts what was a profoundly important *political* moment in the academy, the moment at which the women's movement challenged the ubiquitous misogyny, masculinism, and sexism establishing norms and exclusions in academic research, curricula, canons, and pedagogies. Indisputably, Women's Studies as a critique of such practices was politically important and intellectually creative. Women's Studies as contemporary institution, however, may be politically and theoretically incoherent, and tacitly conservative. It is incoherent because by definition it circumscribes uncircumscribable "women" as an object of study, and it is conservative because it must, finally, resist all objections to such circumscription: hence the persistent theory wars, and race wars, and sex wars, notoriously ravaging women's studies. Theory that destabilizes the category of women, racial formations that disrupt the unity or primacy of the category, and sexualities that similarly blur the solidarity of the category—each of these must be resisted, or worse, colonized, to preserve the realm. Each, therefore, will be compelled to go elsewhere; and women's studies will consolidate itself in the remains, impoverished by the lack of challenges from within, bewildered by its new ghettoization in the academy, a ghettoization produced this time by feminists themselves. There is no such thing as women's studies. Now what?[13]

The overwhelming response to these reflections, from my cultural studies colleagues ostensibly gathered for a day of critical self-reflection, was glowering silence later broken by *sotto voce* hallway denunciations of my presentation as "reactionary" and "collaborationist with the enemy." While attempting to articulate what I took to be something approximating a crisis in women's studies, I had broken the taboo against calling into question the institutionalization of critical political moments inside and outside the academy. The punishment for this breach was moralism at its finest: to reproach the questioning *and* the questioner as politically heinous, hence also intellectually unworthy.

"Speech codes kill critique," Henry Louis Gates remarked in a 1993 essay on hate speech.[14] Although Gates was referring to what happens when hate speech regulations, and the debates about them, usurp the discursive space in which one might have offered a substantive *political* response to bigoted epithets, his point also applies to prohibitions against questioning from within selected political practices or institutions. But turning political questions into moralistic ones—as speech codes of any sort do—not only prohibits certain questions and mandates certain genuflections, it also expresses a profound hostility toward political life insofar as it seeks to preempt argument with a legislated and enforced truth. And the realization of that patently undemocratic desire can only and always convert emancipatory aspirations into reactionary ones. Indeed, it insulates those aspirations from questioning at the very moment that Weberian forces of rationalization and bureaucratization are quite likely to be domesticating them from another direction. Here we greet a persistent political paradox: the moralistic defense of critical practices, or of any besieged identity, weakens what it strives to fortify precisely by sequestering those practices from the kind of critical inquiry out of which they were born. Thus Gates might have said, "Speech codes, born of social critique, kill critique." And, we might add, contemporary identity-based institutions, born of social critique, invariably become conservative as they are forced to essentialize the identity and naturalize the boundaries of what they once grasped as a contingent effect of historically specific social powers.

But moralistic reproaches to certain kinds of speech or argument kill critique not only by displacing it with arguments about abstract rights versus identity-bound injuries, but also by configuring political injustice and political righteousness as a problem of remarks, attitude, and speech rather than as a matter of historical, political-economic, and cultural formations of power. Rather than offering analytically substantive accounts of the forces of injustice or injury, they condemn the manifestation of these forces in particular remarks or events. There is, in the inclination to ban (formally or informally) certain utterances and to mandate others, a politics of rhetoric and gesture that itself symptomizes despair over effecting change at more significant levels. As vast quantities of left and liberal attention go to determining what socially marked individuals say, how they are represented, and how many of each kind appear in certain institutions or are appointed to various commissions, the sources that generate racism, poverty, violence against women, and other elements of social injustice remain relatively unarticulated and unaddressed. We are lost as how to address those sources; but rather than examine this loss or disorientation, rather than bear the humiliation of our impotence, we posture as if we were still fighting the big and good fight in our clamor over words and names. Don't mourn, moralize.

But here the problem goes well beyond superficiality of political analysis or compensatory gestures in the face of felt impotence. A moralistic, gestural politics often inadvertently becomes a regressive politics. Moralizing condemnation of the National Endowment for the Arts for not funding politically radical art, of the U.S. military or the White House for not embracing open homosexuality or sanctioning gay marriage, or even of the National Institutes of Health for not treating as a political priority the lives of HIV target populations (gay men, prostitutes, and drug addicts) conveys at best naive political expectations and at worst, patently confused ones. For this condemnation implicitly figures the state (and other mainstream institutions) as if it did not have specific political and economic investments, as if it were not the codification of various dominant social powers, but was, rather, a momentarily misguided parent who forgot her promise to treat all her children the same way. These expressions of moralistic outrage implicitly cast the state as if it were or could be a deeply democratic and nonviolent institution; conversely, it renders radical art, radical social movements, and various fringe populations as if they were not potentially subversive, representing a significant political challenge to the norms of the regime, but rather were benign entities and populations entirely appropriate for the state to equally protect, fund, and promote. Here, moralism's objection to politics as a domain of power and history rather than principle is not simply irritating: it results in a troubling and confused political stance. It misleads about the nature of power, the state, and capitalism; it misleads about the nature of oppressive social forces, and about the scope of the project of transformation required by serious ambitions for justice. Such obfuscation is not the aim of the moralists but falls within that more general package of displaced effects consequent to a felt yet unacknowledged impotence. It signals disavowed despair over the prospects for more far-reaching transformations.

· · · ·

What of moralism in intellectual life, represented by what has often been termed "political correctness" inside and outside the academy— a high level of righteousness, defensiveness, and concomitant refusal of the very intellectual and political agonism that one expects to find celebrated in left and liberal thinking? How have commitments to knowledge, questioning, and intellectual depth been overtaken by the kind of fundamentalism historically associated with conservatives?[15] To what extent is moralism within intellectual life a displaced response to political paralysis outside the academy, a paralysis guiltily taken up by and turned back against intellectual life in self-flagellating fashion? Does this anti-intellectual self-flagellation itself substitute for action in the face of despair about action? Or is this moralism a response to an aimlessness within contemporary intellectual life—a feeling of political irrelevance and purposelessness that redoubles some intellectuals' sense of impotence, now experienced both in the political and in the intellectual domains? Precisely what does the moralism specific to contemporary intellectual life symptomize?

A return to the contrast between a substantive moral bearing and its redacted and transmogrified moralistic cousin may help us develop these questions. A richly configured political or intellectual morality bears an openly contestable character insofar as it must be willing to give an account of itself and be tested against other accounts of the good.[16] And it cannot encode itself as law, or in law, without losing its philosophical and spiritual depths—precisely the evisceration that has befallen both liberal and socialist moral doctrine when codified as absolute truth. Moralism, however, is animated by a tacitly antidemocratic sentiment: it does not want to talk or argue but rather seeks to abort conversation with its prohibitions and reproaches. Put another way, while political morality at its best aims to incite a particular political formation and seeks to unite a people under the auspices of the understanding it tenders, moralism takes up and rebukes isolated positions. In this regard, moralism can be understood as a historically specific effect of quite isolated and vulnerable subjects—subjects who claim membership in an abstract identity-based community but rarely experience themselves as concretely sustained or protected by actual communities of solidarity. Similarly, while any particular moral system derives its validity from the possibility that any person might adopt and inhabit it, contemporary political moralism tends to conflate persons with beliefs in completely nonvolunteristic fashion: persons are equated with subject positions, which are equated with identities, which are equated with certain perspectives and values. To be a white woman is thus equated with speaking or thinking *as* a white woman, just as to include a "diversity of perspectives" is equated with populating a panel or a syllabus or an anthology with those who are formally—or, more precisely, phenotypically, physiologically, or behaviorally—marked as "diverse."

Inadvertently, it seems, I have now raised the question of the relationship between moralizing discourse and contemporary cultural or multicultural politics. What makes such politics especially susceptible to a moralizing didacticism? I want to venture four brief and highly speculative answers. First, as counterhegemonic cultural and political formations, they transpire outside the domain of the officially political realm, and in some discursive contrast to that realm's preoccupation with power and interest. Thus, these political formations often understand themselves as truer, as less bound to the corrupting forces of power and interest—in short, as occupying higher moral ground than that of either their putative opposition or their interest group cousins. At the same time, their discursive exclusion by and from the conventional political order constitutes an incessantly repeated injury (thereby redoubling the social injury constitutive of their original formation) that provides the perfect breeding ground for moralism.

Second, notwithstanding the Right's view of them as a monolith, these political formations are so fragmented, are such small elements of movement often so tenuously linked with each other (when they are linked at all), that they invariably assume a siege mentality and see almost all forms of power as a threat to their existence. They are thus susceptible to growing rigidly defensive and brittle out of a sense of their imperiled existence; this defensiveness also tends to preclude their addressing deep sources of injustice and to incite instead a politics that acts at the largely symbolic and gestural level, the level at which moralism runs rampant.

Third, to the extent that identity politics are institutionalized—in academic programs and in political caucuses or other political organizations—they are susceptible to the profoundly depoliticizing logic of liberal institutions: historical conflicts are rendered as essential ones, effect becomes cause, and "culture," "religion," "ethnicity," or "sexuality" become entrenched differences with entrenched interests. But precisely because effects of power have been discursively converted to essentialized entities, their interests cannot be addressed within that discourse. To put this problem another way: identitarian political projects are very real effects of late modern modalities of power, but as effects, they do not fully express its character and so do not adequately articulate their own condition; they are symptoms of a certain fragmentation of suffering, and of suffering lived as identity rather than as general injustice or domination—but suffering that cannot be resolved at the identitarian level. It may be easier to see this dynamic in discourses that essentialize conflict in places such as Northern Ireland, the Middle East, or South Africa. To formulate the problem in those regions as one of Catholics versus Protestants, Arabs versus Jews, or blacks versus whites, rather than understanding the oppositional character of these identities as in part produced and naturalized by historical operations of power (settler colonialism, capitalism, etc.), is a patently dehistoricizing and depoliticizing move—precisely the sort of move that leads to moralizing lament or blame, to personifying the historical conflict in individuals, castes, religions, or tribes, rather than to potent political analysis and strategies. The mechanism is relatively easy to see in cases remote from North American shores; but largely because of the essentializing logic of liberal institutions, such a perspective is much more difficult to sustain when one considers the politics of "cultural diversity"—the depoliticization is in the very appellation—in the United States.

Fourth, and related to the previous point, what travels under the sign of cultural or identity politics often has very little in the way of what neo-Gramscians call a new hegemonic project. By this, I do not mean that "multicultural politics" lacks a proper sense of patriotism, as Richard Rorty has argued,[17] but that it often has no vision of emancipation from racism, homophobia, or sexism (nor a serious analysis of the relationship of these ills to capitalism, and hence to class). Put another way, the problem with a politics of "difference" is that it lacks a vision of the future that overcomes the political significance of such differences, and thus lacks an affirmative collective project. Perhaps it is for this reason that such political formations at times appear more invested in amassing and citing continued evidence of the injury justifying their existence than in figuring alternatives to these conditions (chapter 3 will explore this investment in greater detail). Indeed, where would programs in women's studies or ethnic studies be without the nightmare of gender and ethnic subordination and violation, on the one hand, and the conceit of the analytically isolatable character of these injuries, on the other? Yet these kinds of negative political investments (which themselves signify a form of political paralysis), combined with the bad conscience they foment over the injuries and sufferings of other groups, are sure recipes for moralizing politics. It is as if moralizing filled in the painful and embarrassing blank drawn by so many over the "think globally" side of the post-Marxist imperative to "think globally, act locally." As our global analyses lead us to appreciate the powers constitutive of our current predicament as overwhelming, and as this appreciation stands denuded of the faith that God or Progress will lead us out of this predicament, our local actions reduce to moralistic reproaches—rarely transformations—of the traces of these powers coursing through our immediate environs.

. . . .

If moralistic discourse always harbors a certain anxiety about "practice," it also operates as a strange substitute for action; it is what Nietzsche called "reaction" posing as action. Moralizing is aimed either at prohibiting certain things, words, or deeds or at compelling a very narrow set of words and deeds—and the latter, of course, is also a form of prohibition. Its function is to limit rather than to open, to discipline rather than to incite. This recalls again the anti-intellectual force of moralism, a turn against the intrinsic riches of intellectual life as well as against its particular value for radically democratic practices.

Stuart Hall once characterized the distinction between theory and politics as that between a domain in which meaning is opened up, potentially infinitely, and one in which it is intentionally and strategically arrested.[18] It is the task of theory, he insists, to "make meaning slide," while the lifeblood of politics is made up of bids for hegemonic representation that by nature seek to arrest this movement, to fix meaning at the point of the particular political truth—the nonfluid and nonnegotiable representation—that one wishes to prevail. With due concern for all that such a rough distinction elides, let us ask what happens when intellectual inquiry is sacrificed to an intensely politicized moment, whether inside or outside an academic institution. What happens when we, out of good and earnest intentions, seek to collapse the distinction between politics and theory, between political bids for hegemonic truth and intellectual inquiry? We do no favor, I think, to politics or to intellectual life by eliminating a productive tension—the way in which politics and theory effectively interrupt each other—in order to consolidate certain political claims as the premise of a program of intellectual inquiry. Indeed, we usurp the increasingly scarce space allocated today to thinking, to making meaning slide, as we politicize a space that must in turn guard its borders and mount the barricades to defend the identity it protects. In codifying such a politics as the basis of intellectual life, we ultimately reproduce the reaction of our ostensible opposition as we fix our position, thereby becoming reactionary ourselves. If consolidated representations of identity and truth are the necessary premise of certain democratic political claims, they also necessarily destroy the openness on which the intellectual life required by rich formulations of democracy depends. Can we live with this paradox?

In a remarkable little 1930 essay titled *Politics and Morals*, Benedetto Croce formulated the problematic of politicized theoretical inquiry this way:

Why have I insisted on pointing out, with the greatest care, the distinction between theory and practice, between the philosophy of politics and politics? To urge the philosophers to be modest and not to confuse political life, already sufficiently confused, with inopportune and feebly argued philosophy? Yes of course. . . . But I confess that I was moved, above all, by the opposite desire, namely, to save historical judgment from contamination with practical politics, a contamination which deprives historical judgment of tolerance and fairness. This desire is also, in its own way, politics, profound politics, if what Aristotle, the father of political science, used to say is true, about the contrast between the active and the contemplative life—that not only the actions which turn towards the facts are practical, but even more practical are the contemplations and reflections which have their origin and end in themselves and which, by educating the mind, prepare for good deeds.[19]

Croce here assists us in making an intriguing return to the problematic of morality whose trace I have argued we now experience painfully as the antilife, antipolitical, and anti-intellectual force of political moralism. Yet our return is not a simple recuperation, precisely because we are today forced to openly *invent* our political projects and their moral content, without relying on either teleological or redemptive history, without having recourse to moral or other ontological systems rooted in nature, fetishized reason, the dialectic, or the divine. We are confronted today with the fact of history—and so also with political futures and the actions that would produce and configure them—as a sheer problem of power. This is what is brought into view at the moment that historical metanarratives are fully exposed as fictions.

Croce's argument for a literal and figural separation between political life and intellectual inquiry suggests possibilities both for the rejuvenation of a rich moral political vision and for an abatement of the moralizing by which contemporary intellectual and political formations currently infect each other. To imagine what this stance might look like for intellectuals, consider Foucault's response to an interviewer who asked whether he wrote *The Use of Pleasure* and *Techniques of the Self* "for the liberation movement." "Not for," replied Foucault steadily, "but *in terms of*, a contemporary situation."[20] The difference between "for" and "in terms of" is critical: it indicates whether intellectual life will be submitted to existing political discourses and the formulation of immediate political needs those discourses articulate, or will be allowed the air of independence that it must have in order to be of value *as* intellectual work for political life. Foucault does not position his work with indifference to an existing political movement, nor does he argue that his thinking is unconditioned by it or irrelevant to its prospects. Rather, he distinguishes the value of critical thinking from position taking, policy formulation, or blueprints for action.

Maurice Merleau-Ponty made a similar argument while quarreling with Jean-Paul Sartre about the relevant level of engagement with politics by philosophers.

> I have in no way renounced writing about politics. . . . With the Korean War, I made the decision—and this is something entirely different—to stop writing about events as they occur. . . . In times of tension, taking a stand on each event . . . becomes a system of "bad faith." . . . That is why on several occasions I suggested in this journal [*Les Temps Modernes*] that we present comprehensive studies rather than hastily taken positions. . . . This method is closer to politics than your method of continuous engagement. That in itself makes it more philosophical, as it creates a distance between the event and our judgment of it, defusing the trap of the event.[21]

The trap of the event, to which we might today add the "trap of existing discourses," is precisely that which intellectuals who aim to be thoughtful and useful to political life need to spring open; Foucault (in a formulation elaborated in chapter 6) similarly calls for a critique of the political rationalities organizing existing events and political claims, a critique that can occur neither inside the terms of "the event" nor inside an existing array of political and subject positions. Yet both Foucault and Merleau-Ponty also insist that to argue for a separation between intellectual and political life is not to detach the two. The point instead is to cultivate among political intellectuals an appreciation of the productive, even agonistic, interlocution made possible between intellectual life and political life when they maintain a dynamic distance and tension. By itself a political act at a time when universities are increasingly underwritten by "interested" corporate, private, and state funds, such cultivation is also quite possibly a route to freeing political life from its current moralizing despair and intellectual life from the grip of bad conscience. In the effort to revitalize left politics with rich genealogies, discerning institutional analyses, and compelling political visions, intellectuals who are deeply learned, imaginative, and independent can be of enormous value. But to the extent that critical thinkers in the academy are caught in the dehistoricizing, depoliticizing, and intellectually stifling political moralism spurred by the political disorientations of our time, we will be not be available for this work. As I argue in chapter 7, to the extent that we do not come to terms with the losses generating this moralism, we will remain captive to a melancholy that rehearses it. We will thus be of little help in forging alternatives to those bankrupt trajectories in whose ghostly orbit contemporary political life spins. It is in this spirit of inquiry— one unmoored from the demand for immediate political solutions, a demand that will always sacrifice the riches intellectual life can offer to politics—that the ensuing chapters are written.

■ ■ ■ ■

THREE

DESIRE

The Desire to Be Punished:
Freud's " 'A Child Is Being Beaten' "

Conscience and morality arose through overcoming, desexual-
izing, the Oedipus-complex.
   —Freud, "The Economic Problem in Masochism"

. . . the being beaten also stands for being loved . . .
   —Freud, " 'A Child Is Being Beaten' "

In our time, to consider the desire to be punished may seem
esoteric or self-indulgent when compared to investigations of its apparent opposite, the manifest desire to punish. Early in the 1990s, the
people of California voted to make an offender's third conviction for
felony drug possession carry an automatic sentence of life imprison-
ment. The 1993 Singapore caning of a young American graffiti-writing
vandal inspired several members of California's assembly, "fed up
with crime," to sponsor legislation requiring public paddlings of California youths guilty of petty vandalism. In that same decade, while
slashing education, welfare, and municipal budgets to unprecedented
and inhumane lows, California lawmakers increased spending *only* on
prisons, allocating astounding sums to build them, staff them, secure
them, and populate them. And throughout the United States, the
clamor for public executions of criminals—including the reinstate-
ment of execution by firing squad—continues unabated. Such fierce
passions for punishment, and especially for its display, recall
Nietzsche's formula: "As the power and self-confidence of a community increase, the penal law always becomes more moderate; every
weakening or imperiling of the former brings with it a restoration of
the harsher forms of the latter."[1] Indeed, a better indicator of civic

decline than the rising crime rate is a public apparently more blood-thirsty for punishment of its most marginal citizens than for political or economic justice for the many.

There may be another symptom to be read here as well: a turning away from the difficult work of freedom—work that is risky in its transformative relation with the past, its encounter with power, and its venture into making an uncontrollable future. The retreat from a formulation of citizenship as concerned with the project of producing democracy might well be animating not only the wish to punish others but also a certain wish to be punished, a wish to restage rather than escape scenes of subjection and violation.[2] This chapter considers the second symptom, focusing on the historically specific desire to be pun-ished—not for crimes as such, but for what might be termed the "so-cial crimes" of being female, colored, or queer in a sexist, racist, and homophobic social order that also is acutely conscious of and has fash-ioned a sophisticated set of critical discourses about these injustices. The questions animating my inquiry are these: If subordination or injury through these markings is not simply a matter of political op-pression or repression producing a certain kind of social positioning, but instead entails an ongoing process of subject formation, to what degree might that process include the generation of desire for the inju-rious and punitive social treatment its subjects also decry? What would such treatment confirm, allay, or release in psychic and political identity created at the site of the social rejection or subordination? And how is the reception of such punishment staged—especially through displacement onto others—in a manner that disguises what otherwise might be seen as masochistic political desire consequent to subordinate subject formations? Alongside these historically and cul-turally specific questions about identity formation and political de-mands is another of more general concern: If desire is not inherently emancipatory—that is, if contemporary understandings of subject for-mation no longer allow us to view desiring subjects as desiring their freedom and well-being (including mere freedom from suffering)— from what source is an emancipatory future to be drawn?[3] What might be the ontological supplement or replacement for liberatory desire in the modernist subject's imagined act of will for a better future?

Of course, the modern subject has never been able to rely on desire alone in journeying toward the promised land. At modernity's birth, Hobbes insisted that desire could make a wreck of interests, that only desire harnessed to reason could keep us from the self- and other-destruction that our boundless passions could incite. But even in Hobbes, let alone the gentler liberals such as Locke and Mill, there is no suggestion of an overt desire to be subjected. To the contrary, insofar as our primordial passion is thought to center on individual license to do what we will, we have to be converted to the benefits of being governed and ordered by rules: we have to be persuaded to sacrifice our originary impulse to freedom and self-satisfaction in order to gratify our long-term interests in survival, property, and security. (Hence Hobbes's play on the word *de-liberation* as a device for corralling and organizing desire by reason, for the project of covenanting for the state.) And in the left tradition from Marx to Marcuse, the presumption of a subject born with a passion for freedom—self-realizing in work and self-legislating in society—is also unquestioned, no matter how fraught the path to gaining that freedom. A counterpoint to this modernist confidence in the desire for freedom is offered by the line of thought that runs from Nietzsche to Weber, cresting in Foucault's theory of subjectivization. But have we faced the extent to which this counterpoint depletes a crucial source of the progressivist vision, rooted not in the rationality of the liberal state or in the reasoning capacities of the modernist subject, but in the nature of the liberal subject's desire itself?

In exploring this question, I revisit Freud's 1919 essay " 'A Child Is Being Beaten.' " My purpose with this text is not to psychologize political life directly nor to reflect on the ways that sexual life bears on political life, but rather to allegorize a historical-political problem through the story of desire and punishment that Freud constructs. Freud, of course, is concerned with the ahistorical, transcultural formation of masochistic desire in the Oedipal context, while my aim is to reflect on the ways that problematic—disappointed, illicit, or otherwise unlivable—attachments function as a historically specific constraint upon emancipatory practices. This difference in focus argues against trying to apply Freud's text politically; nevertheless, elements of his analysis may help us understand a particular formation of social identity that encourages punitive reaffirmations of its own sources of suffering.

. . . .

Freud opens " 'A Child Is Being Beaten' " by musing on the frequency with which those being analyzed for hysteria or obsessional neurosis confess to indulging in the fantasy named in the essay's title. Given its frequency, he suggests, the fantasy is probably common in others not manifestly ill and thus "not obliged to confess it."[4] Freud makes several other initial observations. The fantasy has feelings of pleasure attached to it and is repeatedly reproduced for sexual gratification. Yet, as the grammatical form in which it is reported makes clear, the fantasy is, at first presentation, notably ambiguous and vague, without a clearly identifiable subject or object. Confession of the fantasy, he adds, is accompanied by unusually intense shame or guilt—"perhaps more strongly excited in this connection than when similar accounts are given of memories of the beginnings of sexual life" (p. 132). Finally, like other fantasies and fixations that take shape in the child's fifth or sixth year, the fantasy appears not to be rooted in a specific trauma but to issue from "commonplace" and "unexciting" impressions that "provided an opportunity of fixation . . . for precisely that sexual component which was prematurely developed and was ready to spring forward" (p. 110). In short, this fantasy has an ordinariness and frequency about it that is incommensurate with the extreme shame accompanying its confession and is also at odds with the language of perversion in which Freud himself casts it.

From his analysis of four female patients (two instances of the fantasy in males are bracketed until the end of the essay), Freud concludes that the fantasy proceeds through three successive phases of early childhood. The first phase is reported through the indefinite and indirect statement "a child is being beaten": most significant here is that the beaten child is *not* the one fantasizing the scene. Neither, however, is the fantasizing child doing the beating, which is performed by "an adult" who only later will become recognizable as the child's father

(p. 113). Since the fantasizing child is neither agent nor object of the beating, Freud concludes that the fantasy in its earliest phase is neither masochistic nor sadistic; it is not even clearly sexual. Rather, he interprets this phase as the staging of a frank gratification of sibling jealousy that could be represented by the more explicit utterance "my father is beating the child whom I hate" (p. 113). The question Freud leaves unasked, however, is why the fantasy does not emerge in this form, functioning instead through abstraction from the punitive father and despised sibling. What gratification does this abstraction enable that Freud's explicit formulation would foreclose? What crucial ambiguity does it place in erotic, or at least pleasurable, suspension? And how might this abstraction represent a *formation* of desire and subjectivity, and not merely a desire for the specific displacement of a specific sibling from a specific parent's affections?

[The second phase of the fantasy explicitly features the beating of the fantasizing child and is simply expressed: "I am being beaten by my father."] However, this phase, which Freud identifies as "unmistakably of a masochistic character," is "never remembered, it has never succeeded in becoming conscious. . . . It is a construction of analysis" (pp. 113–14).[5] This phase issues from two related but distinct precipitations of guilt: guilt about the desire for the beating of a sibling, and guilt produced by the repression of incestuous love for the father. Yet even as Freud insists that "a sense of guilt is invariably the factor that transforms sadism into masochism," he also argues that guilt alone is not the "whole content of masochism" but must be complemented by the "love-impulse." Thus, the illicit "my father loves me" (and only me) turns (regresses) into "my father is beating me," such that being beaten becomes "a meeting-place between the sense of guilt and sexual love": "*[The beating] is not only the punishment for the forbidden genital relation, but also the regressive substitute for it*, and from this latter source it derives the libidinal excitation which is from this time forward attached to it. . . . Here for the first time we have the essence of masochism" (pp. 117–18). Freud's reading of this "unreal" second phase suggests that the punishment for an unacceptable desire in its own way gratifies the desire. The punishment also sustains the unacceptable desire by providing a substitute for it, a substitute that becomes the lived form of the attachment. Masochism thus takes shape as a means of managing guilt and self-beratement by incorporating them into love and desire, respectively; it is a means of negotiating unacceptable attachments without sacrificing them.

The third phase of the fantasy returns to the vagueness of the first with regard to both the beating's agent and object. But it returns with a difference: in this phase, a group of children (invariably boys) are now being punished, and other kinds of punishments and humiliations may now be substituted for the beating. Moreover, Freud argues that notwithstanding the vagueness of subject and object, this phase has "strong and unambiguous sexual excitement attached to it, and so provides a means for onanistic gratification" (p. 114). This phase, I shall argue, offers a politically developed moment in the punishment fantasy, because of its dispersed identification with the beaten subjects (many other children); its substitution of teachers, headmasters, or other unspecified authorities for the father; and its scene of the (privileged) boys being humiliated while the (socially subordinated) girl looks on.

While claiming that this third phase may carry the most explicit sexual excitement and may also be the fantasy that persists through adulthood, Freud sees it not as a culmination but rather as a cover for the second, masochistic phase. Indeed, for Freud, proof of the supreme importance of the second phase is that it "continues to operate through the agency of the phase that takes its place" (p. 123). Nor does Freud believe that the apparent sadism in the third phase should be taken at face value:

> It appears as though in the phrase, "My father is beating the other child, he loves only me," the stress has been shifted back on to the first part after the second part has undergone repression. But only the form of this fantasy is sadistic; the gratification which is derived from it is masochistic. Its significance lies in the fact that it has taken over the libidinal cathexis of the repressed portion and at the same time the sense of guilt which is attached to its content. All of the many indeterminate children who are being beaten by the teacher are, after all, nothing more than substitutes for the child itself. (p. 119)

As Freud tells it, both the chain of substitutes employed to cover the masochistic fantasy and the conundrums of love and guilt that incite it are quite elaborate. Not only do the other children stand in for the fantasizing child, but a conscious fantasy is substituted for an unconscious one and boys are substituted for the fantasizing girl. (Freud speaks of the fantasizing girls as "changing their sex" and "turning into boys" [p. 124].) Elsewhere, Freud compares these substitutions with the "artistic superstructure of day-dreams" that "had grown up over the masochistic beating fantasy" in two of his patients; their function was to "make possible a feeling of gratified excitation, even though the onanistic act was abstained from" (p. 118). Now, even masturbation has been subjected to the substitutions mandated by guilt-ridden desire's need for a cover-up.

Freud's analysis of the beating fantasy can be summarized as follows: The erotic or pleasurable fantasy of "a child being beaten" begins as a jealous love-fantasy but soon undergoes a combination of repression and regression that turns it in a masochistic and sexual direction. Guilt, overdetermined in its sources, is the mechanism of the turn. While calling this masochistic moment of the fantasy the most important one (albeit later repressed and generally inaccessible to the conscious mind of the adult analysand), Freud reminds us that it is already engaged in managing another repression: incestuous desire. This masochism, which incites its own distress and guilt, generally produces a third phase in which the masochistic desire to be punished as a means of confirming and preserving illicit love is distributed onto others with whom we identify while appearing to passively "look on." The third phase seems at first to convert the masochism of the second phase into sadism once again. However, Freud does not argue that such a transformation occurs; rather, this phase operates as an "artful cover" for an enduring masochistic resolution of illicit love. In fact, all the apparently distinctive phases of the fantasy resolve into one familiar Freudian story: Oedipal conflict is managed by substituting punishment for love and is lived in the form of punishment *as* love. We turn now to politics.

. . . .

Why study masochism, and this particular story about masochism, to inquire into elements of contemporary political life? This text compels our interest for two reasons. First, and most important, it concerns an experience that is initially counterintuitive: a pleasurable fantasy in which the fantasizing subject or the subject's peers are punished by an enemy—the arbitrary, disciplining, omnipotent adult world. In thus representing at the very heart of desire a broken solidarity with oneself and/or one's compatriots, the fantasy represents a constraint on self-regard, a constraint on alliance, and a constraint on the urge for freedom represented by the pursuit or practice of desire. If such a configuration of desire has any analogy in political subject formation in late modernity, we would do well to diagnose and address it. Second, this particular text foregrounds ambiguity in the play of thwarted desire: notwithstanding Freud's effort to order and systematize this play into various phases, the desire to be punished or to punish others is not fixed; nor are the two opposed to each other. " 'A Child Is Being Beaten' " offers one of Freud's clearest statements of the slippery and perhaps misnamed (as "sadism" and "masochism") configurations of the complex of desires to punish and to be punished, to subordinate and to be subordinated, to deliver and to receive pain.[6]

Now, I want to leave Freud's specific cases and purposes and allow a set of political possibilities to unfold inside the framework of desire that Freud offers in his essay. What if the ideal of a just, egalitarian polity and social order promised by liberalism is considered as an object of illicit love for late modern subjects politicized through contemporary identitarian formations? This ideal would be a site of love because it is the foundational frame of hope and possibility for a liberal subject; it would become illicit once the falseness of the foundational frame is revealed. Thus, the process of politicization—in which this egalitarian ideal is shattered—could be viewed as analogous to what Freud insists is at the bottom of the beating fantasies, namely the Oedipal complex. Such an analogy could be found in the discovery, by those pejoratively marked along lines of gender, sexuality, or race, that the world to which they had presumed they belonged, and to which their fealty and passion are originally directed, did not in fact hold them in esteem: it spurned their expectations of belonging and protection, thereby humiliating them in their attachment. If identity for marked subjects in late modern liberal orders coincides with this sort of discovery, if politicized identity "occurs" at the point where the liberal promise of universal personhood (and all of its attendant goods) is found hollow, might the injury foundational to such identity contain not simply jealousy and disappointment but also persistent, yet thwarted, desire? And might such jealousy and desire travel paths analogous to those mapped by Freud in his essay on fantasies of beatings?

In this vein, let us consider three possible interpretations of the relationship between the particular formation of late modern political consciousness rooted in identity and the potential desire for reaffirming that identity through punitive social acts of racism, sexism, and heterosexism. In the first reading, we begin with the premise that identity rooted in injury is not achieved through a single act or experience but must be reenacted or reaffirmed over time. Indeed, there is probably no better testimony to this than its apparent counterexample: identity rooted in a traumatic past. To make, for example, the surviving of incest into an identity, to make the past into the subjective and objective present, one has to reiterate the injury discursively, emotionally, as bodily and psychic trauma in the present. One has to establish that the injury lives, that the trauma is repeated not only through the subject's psychic and bodily distresses but also through its denials and dismissals by others. More intuitively, identities based on gendered or racial injury cannot rely on some distant past of pain: for gender or race to be continuous sources of identity, repeated acts of sexism and racism must occur in the present and immediate context of the subject.

Yet suffering the injury required for and constitutive of identity on one's own body or psyche is explicitly and nonpleasurably painful. Who would intentionally seek such a thing, even if one's identity depended on it? To avoid this pain, one might locate that repetition outside oneself—but in those with whom one closely identifies. A certain nonsadistic gratification is thereby obtained through the specter of the victimization of "one's people." Indeed, this is how the figure of an abused and exploited Linda Marchiano (Linda Lovelace in the 1972 porn film *Deep Throat*) appears to operate in the feminism of Catharine MacKinnon; it is, more generally, how MacKinnon's litanies of women's sexual victimization appear to function in her writing: MacKinnon makes a repeated rhetorical gesture at erasing the lines between the stories of sexual violation she recounts, herself, and the reader. A similar reading explains a popular bumper sticker of the early 1990s, "Anita Hill is every woman"—a statement whose patent falseness (especially in its eschewal of the complexities of race in the United States) precisely converges with its cathartic reaffirmation of universal female victimization. And how else can we understand a certain iconographic rendering of Rodney King's brutal beating by Los Angeles police and the endless media replay of the repeated blows to his body, as well as the repetition of those blows—received and delivered—in the riots following the initial trial that exonerated his assailants? Or think of the effect of the 1998 murder of gay college student Matthew Shepard in consolidating the identity of gay students as persecuted. The narrative structure of several of the essays within *Words That Wound* (a volume arguing for the regulation of racist hate speech) and Catharine MacKinnon's *Only Words* also exemplifies this move: specific injuries to specific individuals are cast in the openings of these texts to rhetorically convey their generalized experience by members of the target groups.[7]

If the staging of punishment against one's peers confirms identity rooted in injury without making the subject suffer the injury directly, then presumably this displacement also spurs guilt that itself must be assuaged or expiated. At the same time, this guilt would disrupt the identification with those on whom the blows land, thus rendering the displacement less effective and inducing a new set of anxieties about the identity whose affirmation is sought. Moreover, the guilt would produce its own new economy of obligation and aggression toward the suffering and toward the world that induced that suffering.

The oft-remarked tendency toward "victimization" as the dominant modality of contemporary political discourse, a tendency that leads even those who do not appear overtly victimized to claim victim status, might be understood as having one of its sources in a complex need within postliberal identity formations to see and cite victims outside oneself who can stand in for oneself. This need produces the guilty imperative to appear as a victim but does not resolve the guilt driving that imperative. Indeed, guilt about having avoided the worst suffering

that the target group might experience may produce its own desire
for punishment (recall Freud's repeated insistence that *guilt* is what
converts sadism into masochism), as well as anger—guilt's ancestor
and offspring—toward those with whom one seeks to identify and
claim solidarity. This anger itself generates more guilt. The ultimate
result is a political-psychic economy that produces a surplus of scenes
of victimization. Nor do these formations of victimization invite easy
redress: the psychic investments in them are high, blocking smooth
transformation; and the solidarity required to resist victimization is
itself broken by the suffering displaced onto others and then resent-
fully, guiltily, taken up for oneself.

A second possible reading of the relation between politicized identity and the desire to be punished brings us still closer to Freud's essay.
If identity formed at the point of injury is identity formed in part out
of trauma, then there would also be a certain reassurance, and possibly
even erotic gratification, in restaging the injury, either at the site of
our own bodies (masochism) or at the site of another (displaced masochism in which we are split off from that with which we identify as
we are "passively looking on," to use Freud's phrase). Such restaging
stabilizes an identity whose traumatic formation would render unstable its political or public face; it forges a politically coherent, continuous, and conscious identity out of conflicting unconscious desires. In
so doing, it also sustains us in imaginary community with others "of
our kind" in an era when such community is infrequently *lived* in the
form of concrete associations, institutions, and political practices.

However, restaging the trauma that has mixed love and pain, attachment and suffering, also gratifies the complex erotic formation
located at the point of an injured identity's "fall" (from membership in
a universal citizenry, from formal equality, from liberal personhood),
the very point that is the site of such an identity's creation. The moment at which inequality or subordination is first apprehended is inevitably ambivalent—involving loss on the one hand, and a certain relief
from a previously unnamable suffering on the other. In the process of
politicizing one's identity as a woman, as black, as a lesbian, in the
process of losing the world one imagined to be fair, good, and replete
with self-affirming recognition, one also comes to know why one has
suffered rejection or invisibility and can thus depersonalize, indeed

politicize, that suffering. But restaging the trauma of suffering reassures us that what we need or love—the social order that originally hurt or failed us but to which we were and remain terribly attached—is still there. In short, reliving a certain punishing recognition reassures us not only of our own place (identity) but also of the presence of the order out of which that identity was forged and to which we remain perversely beholden. The repetition gratifies an injured love by reaffirming the existence of the order that carried both the love and the injury.

A third way of reading the relation between identity and a desire to be punished focuses our attention on the guide Freud provides for understanding the inseparability of sadism and masochism, aggression and guilt, wounded narcissism and the desire to inflict wounds on others. Freud speculates that the fantasy "a child is being beaten" occurs at a point of oscillation between sadism and masochism, aggression and guilt. Sometimes, Freud claims, the fantasy participates in neither pole of feeling; sometimes in both. One could extend Freud's speculation further by noting that the formulation's grammar, which he refers to as vague, in fact rather precisely expresses (even as it covers) this oscillation by obscuring not only the agent and object of the beating but also the relationship of both to the fantasizing child. Who is the child being beaten? Who is doing the beating? Is the gratification in the scene obtained, at least in part, through abstraction from the particulars, some of which carry the very ambivalence whose resolution would foreclose the gratification? Put another way, do scenes of social punishment for a marked identity broker a complex and largely unexcavated relationship between identity and guilt on one side, and identity and aggression on the other? And if these opposing (yet mutually constitutive) impulses *require* the oscillation between punishing and being punished that is suggested by Freud's three-phase interpretation of the "child is being beaten" fantasy, if these dual impulses keep alive a certain investment in marked identity, are they also a source of political paralysis, a constraint on a subject's willingness to surrender this investment? If so, might they also constrain the desire for emancipation from the injuries that constitute the identity, insofar as they require the incessant restaging—in abstract, ambivalent, and, above all, oscillating terms—of scenes of punishment?

To reflect further on these themes, let us reconsider each of the three phases of the beating fantasy, framing them now as scenes within rather than as progressive stages of the fantasy. The first phase, in which an unspecified child is being beaten by an unspecified adult, and which Freud initially links to the most common formulation of the adult fantasy, affords us an opportunity to reflect on how a certain kind of abstraction functions in psychic and political life. In the specific formation of politicized identity that we have been considering, a move to abstraction appears in the redistribution of agency and punishment onto substitutes. But this abstraction is then retreated from as punishing or injurious structures are personified so that they can be blamed: the sufferer is necessarily abstract, while the agent is necessarily concrete. In fact, the grammar and content of this scene indicate one way in which abstraction from the original site of injury and displaced personification of the source of injury together form a strange literalism: even as the original (ambivalent) occasion for retribution is obscured by the psyche, even as both the source of love and the source of rivalry inciting such retribution fade into generic scenes of punishment, the psyche orchestrates a new scene of culpability and punishment through which unambivalent satisfaction is possible. Put differently, if, as Freud argues, the desire to punish issues from felt impotence or disregard, if it issues from guilty or unrequited love, then the punitive desire is an inherently ambivalent one insofar as it installs (relatively impotent) violence at the site of a hoped-for tenderness and capaciousness. But this original attachment can be preserved through staging the scene of violence in simultaneously abstract and graphic fashion: "a child is being beaten," "a woman is raped every six seconds in this country," "in the time it takes you to read this paragraph, ten children will die of hunger," and so on. While the graphic scene of punishment gratifies anger at the loved object that has betrayed that love, abstraction from the specific object—"a child," "a woman"—preserves its identity and status as loved. And when particular persons or practices—for example, pornography or hate speech—are held responsible for a whole domain of suffering, the displaced or transposed literalism completes the effect of obscuring and thus protecting the original love.

In the second phase, the fantasy ostensibly becomes explicitly masochistic as the guilty desire for exclusive and inappropriate love finds
its only conceivable outlet in the desire for punishment. Political alle-
gorization of this phase suggests that persistent but unacknowledged
social and political idealizations, now disappointed, may find their
only viable expression in an incessant search for punishment from that
which is idealized. Recall that while Freud argues that this explicitly
masochistic phase is rarely brought to consciousness and is ordinarily
dissimulated through the masking strategies of the third phase, he also
characterizes it as the most important, "not only because it continues
to operate through the agency of the phase that takes its place; but
[because] we can also detect effects upon the character which are directly derived from its unconscious setting" (p. 123). In other words,
not merely a particular configuration of sexual desire but a critical
dimension of a certain personality formation can be traced back to
this phase.

> People who harbor fantasies of this kind develop a special sensi-
> tiveness and irritability towards anyone whom they can put among
> the class of fathers. They allow themselves to be easily offended by
> a person of this kind, and in that way . . . bring about the realization
> of the imagined situation of being beaten by their father. I should not
> be surprised if it were one day possible to prove that the same fantasy
> is the basis of the delusional litigiousness of paranoia. (pp. 123–24)

Now, what if a certain social-political formation parallels the psychic one Freud names? What if, in a political consciousness rooted in
a critique of the ideology of universal liberal principles of equality and
liberty, not simply a critique of but a fall from these principles partly
forms the political personality that develops? Such a formation in
those disenfranchised from liberal principles of equality and liberty by
social markings of race, gender, and sexuality would have two crucial
elements: the shattered idealizations of the principles themselves, and
shattered idealizations of those who are socially dominant—whites,
men, heterosexuals. Taken together, what Freud calls the "special sen-
sitiveness and irritability" toward anyone who can be put in "the class
of fathers" would shift toward anyone in a dominant group *or* uphold-
ing liberal idealism—and especially toward that group or person meet-

ing both criteria. However, of importance here is not only the "easily offended" nature of this personality formation but also the way in which being offended comes to stand for being punished—the "offense" activates "the imagined situation of being beaten by [the loved object]"—and thus provides reassurance that the illicit and problematic object of desire is present. Indeed, if this economy of disappointed or humiliated attachment is a site not merely of sexual formation but also of political identity formation, then the need for such a set of idealizations in constituting political identity cannot be overstated. But neither can we underestimate the depth of guilt about these various idealizations and attachments and the political paralysis that results from this constitutive moment.

Here Freud's story converges in some ways with Nietzsche's account of "the eagerness and inventiveness" on the part of "the suffering" for "discovering occasions for painful affects" and "dwelling on nasty deeds and imaginary slights."[8] Yet Freud goes beyond Nietzsche in seeing the source of such litigious mentalities in broken or impossible love rather than in the generic suffering of the oppressed or weak. Freud's analysis also departs from Nietzsche's in characterizing the desire to be punished (here framed as the incessant discernment and negative mobilization of "offensive" words or actions) as a means of sustaining love, while Nietzsche identifies this impulse with a spirit of revenge against the strong by the weak. The difference between Freud's attention to the animating love behind the hatred and Nietzsche's reification of the hatred (resulting from resentment) is a critical one, especially when considering how to intervene in this dynamic in order to loosen the grip of the political masochism it incites. With Freud's analysis in hand, we can conceive of psychologically transforming and politically mobilizing the disavowed love and idealization that is fueling the rage at the offense. This mobilization might take shape as a certain ironic ethos or as a spirit of radical, critical patriotism—or it might take some other form, as yet unthought.

The political face of the third phase is possibly the most familiar. In this phase, a desire to be punished is distributed onto others such that it does not appear as one's own desire but rather as the inevitable fate of the punished, the wretched of the earth, the downtrodden. But it is also here that love of the object itself is almost completely disguised, as the object is rendered mercilessly punitive. This kind of sensibility appears in certain contemporary narratives of seamless, persecutory racism or sexism: "It cannot be coincidence," more than a few interviewees were reported to reflect as the O. J. Simpson story broke, "that three black male icons, Michael Tyson, Michael Jackson, and O.J., have all been taken down in the past year." Here, too, one may locate the incessant whine of certain American left-liberal publications about quite routine and predictable corruptions of state, cruelties of capitalism, and outrages of imperialism. It is not the author of such narratives who is being injured but numerous and often nameless others, each of whom could stand in for the narrator. Equally important, in every case one can discern the extent to which the narrative does not simply require the social order it decries but is profoundly attached to it. What would *The Nation* be without the political scandals, intrigues, and atrocities it moralizes against each week and for which it advances no real remedy?

While Freud's third phase bears a familiar political face, it also contains a potentially promising twist, one that Freud seems largely bewildered by even as he reports it. In this phase, Freud muses, the children fantasized as beaten are always boys, regardless of whether the fantasizing children are girls or boys. Since the beaten children are "nothing more than substitutes for the [fantasizing] child itself," Freud concludes that the fantasizing girls "change their sex" and "turn into boys" (p. 124). Explainable neither by generic rivalry between the sexes nor by the sex of the sibling who was originally hated, this phenomenon instead "points to a complication in the case of girls. When they turn away from their incestuous love for their father, with its genital significance, they easily abandon their feminine role. They spur their 'masculinity complex' . . . into activity, and from that time forward only want to be boys. For that reason the whipping-boys who represent them are boys too" (p. 119).

But what if Freud is here ill-served by his assumption that the "whipping-boys" only and always represent the fantasizing girls themselves? What if he has elided something as well in his refusal to grant this "phase" of the fantasy any sadistic standing whatsoever—perhaps even a sadistic standing that does not only have masochism at its core? What if such a fantasy is not only or not at all a muted scene of punishment/love of the girl by her father, but is rather an angry retort by the humiliated feminine psyche to the privileged place of the male, whether brother, father, or—since these scenes are ordinarily drawn from books and school, according to Freud—schoolmates or teachers? If such a reading of this "sex change" is viable, might the scene produce a certain release from the relatively closed economy of guilt and punishment that Freud schematizes? Might it even offer a reprieve by "politicizing" the disappointment spurring the masochistic phase of the fantasy in which longed-for loved is replaced by punishment? Alternatively, such a reading could be located in a Nietzschean frame of suffering's endless quest for revenge: the subordinated girls imagine the beating of little boys as a mode of impotent retaliation against their own subordination. In that case, the fantasy would still be locked in the economy of a punitive response to guilty and disappointed love. It would still be trapped in the narrow oscillation between the desire to punish and the desire to be punished in which guilt is the conduit that switches the one into the other, while freedom, as a wish or a practice, is nowhere to be found.

F O U R

■   ■   ■   ■

POWER
Power without Logic without Marx

Why engage, at this historical moment, in close critical readings of Marx's texts on the topic of power? Why search his thought for internal dissensions and unintended thematics? It seems to me that contemporary left intellectuals—Marxists, post-Marxists, democratic socialists, critical race theorists, and feminist theorists—are often uncertain about how to think about the nature of power even as they are preoccupied with power's effects. Few have completely cashed in a modernist left formulation of power organized by hierarchy, arranged as domination and subordination, and measured by exploitation, for a Foucaultian understanding of power as ubiquitous in presence, microphysical and diffuse in nature, circulating in movement, and producing subjects in its effects. Few have replaced all investment in an empirically based materiality of power with a fully discursive rendering; few have surrendered a belief in power as held by particular groups to view power as producing social positions rather than deriving from them. Fewer still have jettisoned the idea that power works systematically and coherently, through logics of its own. At the same time, most leftists have been influenced, tacitly or explicitly, by post-Marxist accounts of power and can thus be described as working rather awkwardly *between* mutually contradictory conceptions of power. One reason for a reconsideration of Marx, then, is to think through some of the conceptions of power with which we casually, and sometimes incoherently, operate.

This contemporary lack of clarity about power is evident in the debate on the Left about the political value of poststructuralism. In large part, the discussion implicitly turns on the question of power—how it really works, where it is located, what kind of theoretical idiom best captures it—yet rarely is power directly theorized. Most neo-Marxist attacks on poststructuralism fault it for being either unpolitical or unscientific; the two criticisms converge in rejecting a poststructuralist critique of extradiscursive reality and of lawlike courses of events. Against poststructuralist assaults on epistemological objectivity and historical metanarratives, neo-Marxists often assert both a logic of society available to quasi-empirical apprehension and a politics that issues directly from such apprehension. Yet in this assertion, the critique of Marxist formulations of power that poststructuralism advances is rarely addressed forthrightly: the questions of what generates power, where or whether it is held, and how it moves thus go unanswered. In the effort to bring these debates more squarely in line with the terms that organize them, and to substitute argument for denunciation, it may be helpful to reconsider the logics of power in Marx's thinking.

There is a second motivation for this theoretical endeavor. Marx's particular adaptation of the Enlightenment progressivist view of history is compelling in part because it formulates with such precision what moves history—the development, organization, and dynamic of change in modes of production. But if Marx's understandings of the character of history and the character of social power are in this way interlocked, then to question his historiography is also to call into question the logics of power it depends on and supports. Put the other way around, Marx aimed to discern power underneath the cloak of metaphysics—idealist philosophy and classical political economy— that had kept it from view, and at the same time recloaked power with his own materialist metaphysics and historical metanarrative. Marx's brilliance as a critic was to track power where others saw contingency or fate, to supplant the magic of a history propelled by ideas with an articulation of the specific processes that have the capacity to move social relations and develop political forms. As is well known, however, in these dynamics of history—from class struggle to fetters on the mode of production—elements of a Hegelian logic of history persist, including notions of dialectics, contradictions, progress, and unitary forces and aims. Marx's project of demystifying history told in an idealist mode thus inaugurates a new mystery, though one anointed in the secular tonalities of science. Marx's endeavor of demystification itself tells a story about power that aestheticizes it—an aestheticization disguised by the claim to scientific transparency, by the conceit of science's nonideological character.

This chapter therefore extends Marx's own project of demystification of the discourses of power, while recognizing that it will not result, as Marx hoped, in a new, transparent and objective discourse but rather can only reveal some of the operations of truth in the discourses claiming transparency and objectivity. The analysis aims Marx's critique of metaphysical logics of power at the logics of power in Marx, in part to question more generally whether power has a logic or logics, in part to ask whether Marx sustains these logics or if and when they falter, and in part to ask whether he achieves the distinction he seeks between power and critique. Does power move along logical tracks, such as those mapped by discourses of contradiction and dialectics, and by formulas of exploitation and obfuscation? Are these logics tantamount to discursive frames or epistemes, are they orders of norms and deviations, or is something more physical, indeed causal, implied by the very notion of logic or power? Moreover, if power does not have a logical structure or move according to logical sequences, how might power be thought and theorized in a different mien and vein? Does Marx hint at such difference? Where does his own thought exceed and contravene his effort to discern power in scientifically mappable formulas? Finally, what are the generative powers of mystification, and how does Marx's own thought partake of them?

· · · ·

Across the whole of his work, Marx aims to replace the popular and scholarly preoccupation with state and ideological power with a focus on what is most often translated as "social forces." Thus Marx's cognate terms for power include not only "labor" and "capital" (in the later writings) but "multiplied productive force," "real material life," and even "the actual nature of things" (in the earlier writings). Marx understands all forms of political power in inegalitarian orders to be a mediated appropriation of man's "essential powers"—that is, social and, more specifically, productive power. In other words, for Marx political power is always derivative, while social power is conceived as original and self-generating: "All struggles within the State . . . are merely the illusory forms in which the real struggles of different classes are fought out among one another."[1] Here arises the paradox, Etienne Balibar notes, that "in order to reassert . . . autonomy in politics, meaning the self-determination and self-liberation of the people, Marx had to deny the autonomy of the political."[2] Historically, this denial has prevented orthodox Marxist theorists from exhibiting much concern with the political institutions relevant to radical democracy or communism. If there is only one kind of human power, and if it shapes all human associations, then there is little point in tinkering with power's manifestations rather than its source. Political organization is taken to follow social or material organization. In Marx's succinct formulation: "assume particular stages of development in production, commerce and consumption, and you will have a corresponding social constitution, a corresponding organization of the family, of orders or of classes, in a word, a corresponding civil society. Assume a particular civil society, and you will get particular political conditions which are only the official expression of civil society."[3]

Marx understands the sphere of civil society, more specifically the sphere of material life, to be *the* domain of power's operation, and he conceives a focus on this domain as always already a focus on power: "civil society is the true source and theater of all history."[4] Thus, to depict the elements and operations of civil society accurately is to depict the elements and operations of power. Civil society names the domain of power; the social names its ground; human productive activity is its wellspring. Thus to apprehend power, two things are required: a critique of the idealism (manifested in state-centered political reforms as well as in Hegelian philosophy) that both covers and apologizes for power, and a science of materialism.

Yet in transposing Hegel's dialectic from the realm of rationality and the state to the realm of materiality and civil society, Marx appropriates a metaphysics of power that retains the structure of idealism even as it aims to repudiate its content. It is not simply that Marx believed in progressive dialectical movement or in the potency of negation and contradiction, but that he conceived of power as generated through logical entailment and as traveling along circuits of logic; power is neither random nor incoherent, and its effects can be tracked by the logic of its generation. Indeed, for Marx the dynamic and effects, if not the material, of power could be said to consist of logical entailment. This is equally true of the formula for extracting surplus value specified in the labor theory of value, the logic of alienation in labor articulated in commodity fetishism, and the inverting logic of the *camera obscura* constitutive of ideology in class society. But if power is produced out of logical entailment, then logic itself generates power, thereby calling into question power's "material" content at the very moment and through the very theory by which this content is asserted. Moreover, if power is produced out of logical entailment, then Marx's own critique cannot escape its implication in power: it depends on logical entailment and hence forms part of a chain of power, replete with the elements of mystification that Marx insists are an inherent dimension of power undemocratically distributed. Put another way, if power is generated out of logical entailment, then the logics Marx brings to the apprehension of power do not simply read power but generate it. If logic is generative, if it produces, then it never simply describes, which undermines the premise of Marx's scientific critique of power, including his attempt to distance that critique from its object of apprehension. Science will emerge not as an account of power from the outside but as a discourse of power that passes as an external account, and in this passing it mystifies both its own imbrication with power and power as such. Science, and the logics constitutive of it, will turn out to be a source of mystification rather than its solvent.

But, bracketing Marx for a moment, what if power does not operate logically, or perhaps exceeds or escapes the logics generating it? Indeed, why should the material of power in the human world be logic; why should the movement of power be logical? What is our investment, as moderns, in the idea that power follows a logical course? Why should power be orderly and why should it produce order rather than anarchy in the human world? Even if power is potentially maximized through regularization and systems, through producing routine and calculable effects, why should self-maximization be the nature of power? What would give power this aim or this capacity? Even if power had a physicalist dimension that would allow it to follow certain natural (physical) laws of movement and spatial reaction, what would give it a teleological dimension or a temporal logic? What would tether it to purpose and aim in history—indeed, what would give it purpose and aim of its own? And above all, what would serve to unite this physicalist (spatial) and historical (temporal) dimension in a common project? In imbuing power with ontological independence and anthropomorphic ambition, is it possible that Marx ascribed to power a source and form independent of human beings—a natural or physicalist constitution bound to a divine aim—even as he strove to ground both power and history in human activity? At the moment he sought to return history to man, did he supply power with a metahistorical content and course structured by a conception of power's relative autonomy from its human source and objects?

. . . .

To pursue these questions we must first consider the several logics of power that Marx specifies as constitutive of modern societies.[5]

Those who would understand the secret of capitalist accumulation, Marx argues, must turn their attention away from the realm of exchange, where both the classical political economists and popular belief are focused, and toward the realm of production, a little studied and relatively inaccessible place.[6] Marx thereby endorses an ancient distinction between appearance and reality in human affairs, and endorses as well their respective correspondence to surface and depth, popular opinion and philosophical truth, accessibility and relative opacity. This insistence on the importance of descending beneath appearances to find the truth they mask articulates as well both the fundamental move of Marx's philosophical criticism and its putative scientific basis: "all science would be superfluous if the outward appearance and the essence of things directly coincided."[7]

Marx characterizes as derivative, ideological, and obfuscating the domains figured as "the real" in legitimizing discourses: the state, the realm of ideas, the realm of exchange. Conversely, he designates as originary, real, and transparent those domains ordinarily ignored (and considered unpolitical) in theory and popular belief: civil society, the material order, and the realm of production. He not only locates significance in what has been disavowed but spies the apparatus of disavowal in what has been valorized. "It should not astonish us," he remarks about classical economic theory, "that vulgar economy feels particularly at home in the estranged outward appearances of economic relations . . . and that these relations seem the more self-evident the more their internal relationships are concealed from it."[8] Discernible here is a proto-deconstructive impulse in Marx's reversal (but not displacement) of the dualistic constructs (inherited from Hegel and the classical political economists) that he submits to analogical analysis: state/civil society, ideal/material, exchange/production. Each dualism, conventionally construed, is understood to conceal not only the "real order of things" but also the terms of production—the dynamic of power—of that order, and to exist on the basis of that concealment. A focus on and belief in the primacy of the state, ideas, and exchange are precisely what prevent the workings of social power from coming into view. Thus, in the study of capitalism, "we therefore take leave for a time of this noisy sphere, where everything takes place on the surface and in view of all men, and [go] into the hidden abode of production, on whose threshold there stares us in the face 'No admittance except on business.' Here we shall see, not only how capital produces, but how capital is produced. *We shall at last force the secret of profit making.*" Significant for our purposes is both Marx's uncritical appropriation of the problematic philosophical conceit of an essential truth lying beneath deceptive appearances and the logic of power that such a conceit expresses. In Marx's account, power always operates behind a veil and always throws up a surface "in view of all men" that distracts us from its abode; power produces its mystification—it produces a whole order of mystification—as a fundamental rather than incidental effect. This "perversion of reality," Marx suggests, is present in all forms of society that feature commodity production and money circulation, but it is nowhere more completely expressed than under conditions of capitalist production.[10] Because power produces its own camouflage and structure of legitimation through ideology when it is distributed undemocratically, and because capitalism represents the extreme of an undemocratic distribution of power in its division of society into "two great classes directly facing each other,"[11] the "secret" of capitalist power (profit making) must be "forced" through a critical analysis that can undo the reversals with which power covers itself. This process requires that both subjects and objects of power be grasped as effects of power, as fabricated by power, rather than as natural, given, or accidental.

But if subjects and objects of power are always the effects of power according to Marx, why should this cease to be the case when power is no longer maldistributed, when it is shared among rather than held by political economic subjects? For Marx this is the historical moment at which power becomes both legitimate and transparent, no longer requiring dissimulation. In conditions of true equality, social power— its basis in labor and its distribution through society—loses its secretive quality. At this moment, too, subjects recover an essential nature ("species being") that is prior to power. Paradoxically, while a particular (collective and radically democratic) organization of power is a condition of this recovered nature, that organization of power is not cast as constitutive of the subjects themselves. At the very point at which subjects are seen to have fully reclaimed their social powers as their own, power ceases to produce and organize them as subjects. Subjects are returned to their true nature at the moment they are rejoined with one another in a condition of radical interdependence and cooperation—but this return and this rejoining entail a recovery of authenticity and freedom (unalienated species being and true human emancipation) that excludes or evicts power. Thus, the final form of history recovers the relation to power of its prelapsarian ancestor. Marx puts the matter this way: "All-round dependence, this natural form of the world-historical co-operation of individuals, will be transformed by this communist revolution into the control and conscious mastery of these powers, which, born of the action of men on one another, have till now overawed and governed men as powers completely alien to them."[1]

Yet a power fully mastered, fully under collective sway, is a governing power no longer—hence its transparency as well as its impotence in controlling men's lives. Power rendered transparent and impotent, power that no longer overawes or governs, is power that is not power. Thus does power evaporate just as it is collectively grasped, as its historic maldistribution is rectified. So also at the moment they share in it equally do subjects cease being produced by power, organized by power, positioned by power, and, above all, mystified by power. But if power is power only when it is not shared, and hence when it is not transparent, we face two possibilities. Either Marx, as Foucault implies, offers us a scene of emancipation that is beyond and outside power, a picture that is otherworldly in the extreme, a picture that partakes of the same religious logic that Marx sought to reject in his break with Hegel. Or perhaps, in the exhaustive abolition of ownership and individual agency that is required by Marx's formulation of power collectivized, there is an implicit confession that power cannot be completely shared, that democracy is impossible, that communism is an unreachable ideal, precisely because power resists equal distribution—resists equality as such. In either case, Marx appears to tacitly recognize that power shared is no longer power, that the only way to capture power collectively is to deprive everyone of it.[13] (Can what we once called "actually existing communism" be sympathetically understood as impaled on this problem, on the conceit that power can be vanquished from human society?)

Power that exceeds the form of the labor that generates it is, according to Marx, undemocratic by nature (and hence disappears in true democracy); it is also unknowable insofar as it always and necessarily disguises itself, and this disguise is part of what constitutes the power of power. Here, let us return to the passage, cited earlier, in which Marx promises to discern the true nature of capital by violating the private property line protecting its secret. In seeking to discover, in "the hidden abode of production," not only "how capital produces, but how capital is produced," Marx gestures toward a double operation of power: it simultaneously produces itself as a subject or agent and produces an effect outside of itself. The exploitation of labor in commodity production, for example, produces not only capital but also the system of capitalism that reproduces all of the system's elements. For Marx, power produces its own conditions of reproduction and hence its own futurity, although both moments of production are necessarily rife with contradiction. As he explains in *Capital*, "Like all its predecessors, the capitalist process of production proceeds under definite material conditions, which are, however, simultaneously the bearers of definite social relations entered into by individuals in the process of reproducing their life. Those conditions, like these relations, are on the one hand prerequisites and on the other hand results and creations of the capitalist process of production; they are produced and reproduced by it."[14] But how could power achieve such a feat—producing both its necessary prerequisites and its intended effects—without having divine or naturalistic dimensions, a metaphysical structure and a teleological course? And what would give humanly generated power these characteristics? Why should power know where it is going if those generating it, produced by it, steeped in it, are largely clueless about its course? What ghostly remainder of God's prescience and of inherent human ignorance shapes this putative secularization of history? Indeed, not only does Marx ground human social and historical existence in a deep metaphysics, but it is a metaphysics that evaporates at the moment that humans acquire control of their own existence, at the moment they win freedom. Insofar as this freedom entails an emancipation from metaphysics, it is our essential humanness—or, more precisely, our angelic essence—that replaces the structuring function occupied in history by metaphysics.[15]

. . . .

The formulas for exploitation and accumulation that Marx discovered in the "hidden abode of production" are primarily expressed in the labor theory of value, but they involve the logic of commodity fetishism and alienation as well. Though Marx extends and revises Adam Smith's labor theory of value relatively modestly, he replaces a "hidden hand" and "free exchange" with a theory of the systematic exploitation and inequality at the heart of capitalist accumulation. Capital is formed out of surplus labor, that is, labor performed over and above what is necessary to reproduce the worker. Extracted systematically through a combination of lengthening of the working day (increasing the amount of labor power extracted) and technological developments (reducing the proportion of labor required to reproduce the worker), surplus labor is "realized" through the exchange of commodities on the market. "Capital is not sum of the material and produced means of production. Capital is rather the means of production transformed into capital."[16]

A host of contradictions accompany the process of producing and realizing capital—from degrees of exploitation that destroy rather than reproduce workers to the suppression of purchasing power and investment by holding down wages—but in Marx's account such contradictions only serve to affirm the logics themselves. Indeed, the contradictions operate as proof of the systematic nature of the process Marx maps insofar as they demonstrate its organized and bounded nature. Just as the unevenness of historical development explained by dialectical materialism confirms rather than undermines the notion of progress in history, so the contradictions attendant on capitalist production and capital realization confirm rather than undermine the systematic quality of that process.

The specific power in capitalist political economy—that which "produces capital" as well as that which is "produced by it"—is, of course, labor converted into labor power, labor that is first commodified and then purchased, wielded, and exploited by capital. Labor is converted into commodity form when its capacity to provide for itself is removed, that is, by the ubiquity and dominance of capital. Historically, this conversion is achieved through enclosure movements and other social processes that proletarianize workers, depriving them of access to the means of production. Proletarianization is itself the outcome of a certain logic of history, in which the bourgeoisie is generated out of and presses against the fetters of late feudal production: the emergence of this new class configures labor in terms necessary for the realization of its economic and political ascendancy. Such realization requires the production of a class that Marx ironically calls "free" in the double sense of being free *of* the capacity to produce its own subsistence and free *to* sell its labor power on the open market—that is, free from feudal social or political constraints on its movement. To generate a class with this double freedom and a propertied bourgeoisie, the order in which neither property nor labor could circulate freely had to be *politically* transformed: some version of a liberal constitutional order had to be brought into being, one that secured both universal property rights, including property in selves, and bourgeois liberties of movement. Thus, the logic of capitalist accumulation in the exploitation of free labor *entails* the Age of Revolution that bears forth the conditions of such accumulation.

This brief sketch of the major elements of capitalist production suggests that the logics of power constitutive of Marx's political economy form a lengthy interlocking chain in which each element is hinged to a presupposition that is itself another vital element in the chain. On a literal level, "capital is dead labor that, vampire-like, only lives by sucking living labor, and lives the more, the more labor it sucks."[17] However, this paradoxical vampire logic according to which the dead live by sucking life from the living can transpire only within a complex logic of history in which capital is born out of contradictions in feudal production on the one side, and generates its "own gravediggers" on the other. Political economy has internal, *spatially* organized logics of power that generate capital, class, exploitation, commodification, fetishism, and so forth. But political economy is also ordered by *temporal* logics such as those expressed by the terms *contradiction, fetter,* and *development*, the logics that make up Marx's philosophy of history. "Class struggle" is an instance of both combined: it animates political economy in time, and it also opposes the pure temporality of the Hegelian dialectic—it carries the spatial dimension that materialism installs in the dialectical progress of history. Yet the spatial and temporal logics also presuppose one another, a presupposition that effectively cloaks the workings of power precisely where it is meant to be exposed. Put another way, there is a curious shell game at work in Marx's schemes of logical entailment: in a series of effects, each of which comes on the heels of and generates another, where is the animating dynamic in the series? That is, where is power? To the extent that power is not a material substance but a social relation for Marx, and to the extent that disguise is part of its nature, is it inevitable that bringing it literally into view would be impossible, even and especially in a materialist analytic frame? Or is this failure a consequence of a form of critique that hinges power to logic, and its circularities, rather than to a domain and mechanics of uncapturability, relationality, and contingency?

The problematic of alienation may provide a means of addressing these questions. Marx sees alienation as resulting from a particular form of the organization of labor and economic distribution and not, as Hegel insisted, from labor as such (understood as an activity of "externalization"). In this as in many other instances, Marx recasts Hegel's (eternal) anthropological verity as a historically specific production. In capitalist commodity production, commodities acquire a socially oppressive existence and are elements of an economic and social order that is oppressive and exploitative: they come to have a power "over and against man" that is both drawn from and constitutive of the power of capital itself.

Marx makes alienation tell the story of labor that is congealed in an object "foreign" to the worker—produced neither from his intellectual conception nor under his direction and control: "estrangement is manifested not only in the result but in the *act of production*—within the *producing activity* itself."[18] But Marx also makes alienation tell the story of man's psychic estrangement from a human universe that, though he dwells in it, is not under his control. Marx thus employs the notion of alienation to signal the double effect of estranged labor—social powerlessness and psychic deauthentication, estrangement from one's activity and estrangement from one's world—each conditioning the other. In so doing, he is attempting to forge an analytic link between economy and psyche, between mode of production and *habitus*, that exceeds what his formulations of the relation between material life and consciousness ordinarily convey. The recognition that the appropriation of man's labor in capitalist commodity production produces a lived experience of worldly alienation (and not merely alienation from the processor products of his labor) is a recognition that the economic produces the subject not simply as an objective member of a class but *as* subjectivity. How else to read Marx's evocative lament:

> The worker therefore only feels himself outside his work, and in his work feels outside himself. He is at home when he is not working, and when he is working he is not at home. . . . Just as in religion the spontaneous activity of the human imagination, of the human brain and the human heart . . . operates on him as an alien, divine or diabolical activity—in the same way the worker's activity is not his spontaneous activity. It belongs to another; it is the loss of his self. As a result . . . man . . . no longer feels himself to be freely active in any but his animal functions . . . and in his human functions he no longer feels himself to be anything but an animal. What is animal becomes human and what is human becomes animal.[19]

This passage suggests that labor is always more than labor and its tangible effects, and that material life is always more than material—

indeed that it is immaterial, felt, even transubstantial in the way it is lived. This "more than" would seem to exceed Marx's own argument, in *The German Ideology* and elsewhere, that political economy gives rise to a host of relations and associations not directly identifiable as economic—family, state, interstate, religious, and cultural.[20] Rather, the implicit formulation of power here appears to elude Marx's vocab- ulary for describing it, since the psychic formation he hints at is at least as complex as the process of production he maps, and that forma- tion itself participates in, becomes generative of, the process of pro- duction.[21] Had Marx had access to or developed such a vocabulary, however, the logics of power he asserts might well have unraveled: the reverberation of power *between* psyche and economy would likely have undone any logical relation, producing something far less general and temporally well ordered, hence less predictable and progressive. Workers alienated from their labor in a material sense can strike, sub- vert, or even seize the apparatus of production, but what of alienated psyches? Aren't they as likely to act out as act up? Or perhaps even more dispiriting, aren't they as likely to become one with the machin- ery as to throw a wrench in it?

Even within Marx's terms, however, it should be evident that to designate his model of power in production as economic or commod- ity-like, as Foucault does,[22] is to vastly reduce the complexity of his understanding of the effects of commodified, appropriated, and alien- ated labor. While the precipitating moment in this process is the reduc- tion of labor to the commodity as labor power, and the alienation of that commodity from its owner, even this moment is compounded from a much denser operation of power: commodification is itself *achieved* through alienation, and the latter is simultaneously and inter- dependently physical and psychic. Alienation is not merely an effect but a condition of the production of the commodity insofar as it is the condition of commodity fetishism and of the procurement of labor power by the capitalist. Moreover, the logic of power Marx traces in the operation of the commodity is, by his own admission, not a tangi- ble but a "mystical" one, "at the same time perceptible and impercep- tible by the senses." As he elaborates in *Capital*, "the existence of things *qua* commodities, and the value-relation between the products of labor which stamps them as commodities, have absolutely no connexion with their physical properties and with the material relations arising therefrom."[23] In short, Marx treats this kind of power neither as a commodity nor as a material force but as constituted by ideology, or what he here denotes as fetishism. *Pace* Foucault, Marx does not figure this kind of power as a commodity but precisely as a relation that comes to assume commodity form—which is, crucially, the form in which the nature of power is mystified.[24]

And here is the really telling moment in Marx's discussion of commodity fetishism and alienation: while commodity fetishism is an inevitable feature of the capitalist mode of production, while it is an effect of that mode of production, it is also a prerequisite of such production. If commodities were not fetishized, Marx suggests, capitalist production would not be possible. "This I call the Fetishism which attaches itself to the products of labor, so soon as they are produced as commodities, and *which is therefore inseparable from the production of commodities.*"[25] Capitalist exchange requires the mutual exchangeability of goods, that is, the universal emphasis on exchange value over use value that can occur only when all commodities are fetishized. Neither the elements of production (labor), nor the elements of exchange (commodities), nor the currency of exchange (money) could be mobilized without being fetishized. In this regard, the phenomenon of the fetish, a mystical phenomenon, is not only the inevitable effect of capitalist production, a material process, but is also what enables that process. Both cause and consequence, prerequisite and effect, the strange logic of the fetish in Marx appears more paradoxical than even its psychoanalytic cousin whose essential formula, "I know, but still . . . ," conveys an *undulation* inherent in the working of power: power cannot be fully captured by structure or formula because it must move and dissimulate in order to persist. Never linear or sequential, yet essential to the material production of material things, the fetish, according to Marx, can be apprehended only through "recourse to the mist-enveloped regions of the religious world."[26]

It might even be said that the fetish is the consummate form of power for Marx insofar as it mystifies and materializes in the same gesture, insofar as it crystallizes the necessity and inevitability of mystification for materialization. Indeed, if fetishism is that process whereby power as a relation is obscured through reification, through the guise of an object, then what Marx calls material life, with its thoroughly objective, tangible, and concrete character, is always already fetishized. The fetish exemplifies mystification as a mechanism simultaneously producing power as material currency, the power of the commodity, and the power of capital. The fetish is an *operation* of power in a logic that defies both agency and physicality even as it participates in and constitutes both. That power transpires as an operation is crucial to the larger schema that Marx is mapping because it marks power's *spatial* dimension, its production outside of a temporal logic of development and contradiction. This notion suggests again how far from the mark is Foucault's critique of Marxism as a theory of power reducible to "economic functionality."[27]

Commodity fetishism is a necessary and inevitable emotional-psychic figure and function in capitalism. It is necessary because it binds humans to capitalist production and mystifies both the production process and the bind. It is inevitable because "the life process of society"—the dead labor congealed in the commodity—is inherently veiled in an inegalitarian and alienated order. As Marx explains, "The life process of society, which is based on the process of material production, does not strip off its mystical veil until it is treated as production by freely associated men, and is consciously regulated by them in accordance with a settled plan."[28] In short, the logic of commodity fetishism draws on a prior logic in which power is necessarily mystified when it is not collectivized—and at the moment it is collectivized, as we have seen, power mysteriously vanishes. This set of logical entailments is not simply a political mandate but also an ontological one, and to see it clearly, we must move from *Capital* (back) to *The German Ideology* and "The Jewish Question," and thus from the problem of fetishism back to the concept of the *camera obscura*.[29]

· · · ·

In *The German Ideology*, Marx outlines the science of ideology that binds together his philosophy of consciousness and his philosophy of history in a tight, linear logic. These links are clearest in the famous passage articulating the relationship between the activity and the consciousness of men:

The production of ideas, of conceptions, of consciousness, is at first directly interwoven with the material activity and the material inter- course of men, the language of real life. Conceiving, thinking, the mental intercourse of men, appear at this stage as the direct efflux of their material behavior. The same applies to mental production as expressed in the language of politics, laws, morality, religion, meta- physics, etc. of a people. Men are the producers of their conceptions, ideas, etc.—real, active men, as they are conditioned by a definite development of their productive forces and of the intercourse corres- ponding to these, up to its furthest forms. Consciousness can never be anything else than conscious existence, and the existence of men is their actual life-process. If in all ideology men and their circum- stances appear upside-down as in a *camera obscura*, this phenome- non arises just as much from their historical life-process as the inver- sion of objects on the retina does from their physical life process.[30]

If what we see with our eyes, however distortedly, is what is actually in the world, so, too, according to Marx, "consciousness can never be anything else than conscious existence"—it derives from and refers to the reality of our existence. "Existence" thus has the same objective status as the visual domain apprehended by sight. When life is whole, unalienated, and unstratified, Marx argues, the material basis of all consciousness is transparent; when life is alienated, stratified, and con- trolled by alien powers, then consciousness also suffers these effects. As he concludes in *Capital*, "the religious reflex of the real world can . . . only then finally vanish, when the practical relations of every-day life offer to man none but perfectly intelligible and reasonable rela- tions with regard to his fellow men and to Nature."[31]

Crucially, however, the relation between alienated consciousness and life under alienated conditions is not amorphous: with the figure of the *camera obscura*, Marx both explains consciousness' inversion of reality and offers a potential remedy for this inversion, which can be corrected as completely as the brain corrects the inversion of images on the retina. For Marx, the logic of ideology's inversion of reality is just as absolute, just as necessary and inevitable, as the retina's inver- sion of what is seen. In both cases, reality is not randomly distorted but is turned precisely upside down. Moreover, what appears initially as metaphor or homology between vision and consciousness collapses into identity as a contiguity unfolds between the two processes Marx is analyzing. Ideology is not merely comparable to visual process but is itself about ways of seeing. More exactly, it involves a systematic perceptual distortion of the world: it entails *not* seeing what is objectively there to be seen, because to consciousness that objective thereness appears upside down. Ideology is defined by the *systematic* inversion and dissimulation of reality—both its dynamics and its effects—consequent to inequality. Marx's science of critique promises to correct this inversion just as precisely as the brain corrects the retina's inverted image. Thus, the figure of the *camera obscura* (and of the brain righting the image that the retina inverts) turns into a technical formula for the production of distortion in inegalitarian orders and for the mind's correction of this distortion. In the case of vision, the brain is programmed to reverse the retina's inversion; in the case of ideology, the brain requires the help of social science for the proper correction. Here, in an almost parodic insistence on the logical order of things, is the scientific foundation (ideological inversion akin to retinal inversion) of a scientific critique (systematic reversal and displacement of the inversion) of the science of power (systematic mystification of unequal social relations).

Yet this precision, this scientism, cannot be sustained by Marx. For ideology's inversion of reality turns out to produce not a mere metalepsis but a more general dissembling of social dynamics and effects, a dissembling that involves the invention of mystical figures and non-human agents. Thus, for example, in Adam Smith's political economy, a "hidden hand" is said to reconcile individual and common interests; in Hegel's philosophy of the state, the *idea* of the state and the *idea* of freedom realize one another and "transcend" the unfreedom of civil society. This dissembling that exceeds inversion pertains to two crucial differences between sight and consciousness in Marx's understanding. First, in consciousness the brain not only cures distortion but itself produces distortions; and second, consciousness apprehends (or conjures) not simply objects but *dynamics* of social reality, the source and logic of reality's movement and direction, which are themselves hidden from sight, apprehensible only through abstraction from the object world. Marx identifies both elements in *The German Ideology*:

In direct contrast to German philosophy which *descends* from heaven to earth, here we *ascend* from earth to heaven. That is to say, we do not set out from what men say, imagine, conceive, nor from men as narrated, thought of, imagined, conceived, in order to arrive at men in the flesh. We set out from real, active men, and on the basis of their real life-process we demonstrate the development of the ideological reflexes and echoes of this life-process. *The phantoms formed in the human brain* are also, necessarily, sublimates of their material life-process, which is empirically verifiable and bound to material premises.[32]

Marx locates the initial production of ideology in the historically achieved division between mental and manual labor, a division that permits consciousness to "flatter itself that it is something other than consciousness of existing practice" (p. 159) but that also signals a social division of labor that founds class society, and hence the existence of structured inequality. The character of this founding moment suggests that ideology is born both out of a logical need for mystification—the need to legitimize exploitation and inequality—and out of its logical ground, as thought is split off from material production and what was originally whole is sundered. Again, there is, in this regard, a religious logic at work in Marx's own thinking: 'In the beginning . . . we were one, whole, and lived in Truth. . . .' Truth, communism, authenticity, and transparency are conceived as coinciding at the beginning and the end of history.

In the splitting of manual and mental labor, ideology becomes not only necessary but possible: it is this splitting that disembodies consciousness, separating it from bodily existence and experience (as the eye might be separated from the brain), thus allowing ideology to imagine its process and products as independent of material existence. And it is here that Marx seems to posit a very nearly primary alienation rather than one specific to capitalism: man does not experience the world "authentically" or accurately when he does not experience the whole of human activity in his own activity, when his activity is a fragment of a larger social order rather than a microcosm of it. Hence Marx's argument that "the life process of society . . . does not strip off its mystical veil until it is treated as production by freely associated men and is consciously regulated by them in accordance with a settled plan."[33] The religious logic according to which man's original wholeness is now recovered through a rationally achieved and sustained unity with other men allows Marx to fantasize an overcoming of the (generative) element of mystification in power. Once again, it is an image of power transparent, self-revealing, harmless, and fully within the control of those in its field—not an image of power at all. At the culmination of the logic of history, power itself dissolves and ideology goes with it. History as contingency and conditions thwarting particular intention gives way to (a fantastic picture of) life executed according to a deliberate plan. This is an unhistorical life not simply because the logics of political economy, ideology, and religion have come to an end, but because the frame of this life is no longer conceived of as external to the humans living it: our control of life conditions and of life itself is potentially absolute, though paradoxically shaped by a givenness about species being and its realization in communism that compromises this image of absolute control. Not only have historical conditions become transparent, they no longer determine our possibilities.[34]

The division between mental and manual labor undergirds the logic of ideology's inversion of reality in another way as well. The division itself sunders the ideational from the material world—consciousness from existence—and so renders that separation as a commonplace that becomes commonsensical. The division of mental and manual labor, we have already seen, becomes the basis on which consciousness, philosophy, religion, and the like each flatters itself that it has an independent existence. This division, in short, *generates* the splitting off of consciousness that in turn generates "independent" intellectual life—which presumably comprises not just philosophy and religion, but also natural and social science. Moreover, the domination in the relation articulated by the division is expressed through the appearance of the autonomy of mental labor as natural. In this way, the division between manual and mental labor functions as both the prerequisite to and the ongoing condition of an ideological construction of an inegalitarian social order. Ideology represents the perspective of mental labor that does not grasp its participation and location in a division of labor; this is tantamount to a mind that does not grasp its lodging in a body and a history—precisely, for Marx, the condition of the philosophical or religious mind. Thus do ideology and philosophy, ideology and religion necessarily, rather than accidentally, coincide in Marx's critique of them.

When mental labor is separated from manual labor, mind's idealist conceit about the constituent elements and order of social life is not entirely wrong from a political angle. The ruling class sees the world from the perspective of its disembodiment—the separation of its members' minds from their bodies as well as from the social body of production. Marx's description of the political result is well known: "The ideas of the ruling class are in every epoch the ruling ideas. . . . The ruling ideas are nothing more than the ideal expression of the dominant material relations, the dominant material relationships grasped as ideas; hence of the relationships which make the one class the ruling one, therefore the ideas of its dominance" (p. 175). In sum, disembodied consciousness, a social position of domination, and the very production of idealist thought and philosophy strictly converge. But crucially, this convergence, which is an effect of the division of labor, is also generative:

> Once the ruling ideas have been separated from the ruling individuals and, above all, from the relationships which result from a given stage of the mode of production, and in this way the conclusion has been reached that history is always under the sway of ideas, it is very easy to abstract from these various ideas "*the* idea," the notion, etc. as the dominant force in history and thus to understand all these separate ideas and concepts as "forms of self-determination" on the part of *the* concept developing in history. (p. 174)

The belief that ideas have a dynamic and trajectory of their own is the inevitable outcome of an order in which the "real" elements of material life are disguised, and in which consciousness is regarded as a wellspring rather than an effect of history. "[A]ccording to their fantasy, the relationships of men, all their doings, their chains and their limitations are products of their consciousness" (p. 149).

Idealist philosophy is not only logically entailed by the division between manual and mental labor; it also assists in legitimating that division, and the inegalitarian order it inaugurates, insofar as it under-girds an ideological formulation of the state. Again, a relation that at first appears merely homological emerges as a chain of power relations. In other words, Marx's argument that idealism is to materialism as the state is to civil society (and heaven is to earth) in a structural sense goes beyond homology or analogy: for him, the state's occupation of the space of political life in modernity is a specifically idealist conceit, predicated on the illusion that ideas or principles concerning liberty and equality are the site at which these principles are enacted. The equation of the constitutional state with the political is further premised on the notion that values such as equality and liberty are secured by their abstraction from the concrete dimensions and activities of social life, by their removal from the (material) orders of life that constitute its lived particularity. The universalist reach of the state, and of idealist claims about "man," "freedom," and so forth, thus both results from and legitimates the division of mental and manual labor in class society. In the wake of this division, consciousness fantasizes not only its independence but its universal status—in part because it imagines its thoughts to be independent of any body, time, or lived situation and in part because universalism is the necessary political claim of a class contesting for hegemony. "For each new class which puts itself in the place of one ruling before it, is compelled . . . to represent its interest as the common interest of all the members of society, that is expressed in ideal form: it has to give its ideas the form of universality" (p. 174).

There is yet another respect in which the division of mental and manual labor and of ideas from material life *entails* rather than simply corresponds to an ideological formulation of state and civil society. Marx argues that the state *as such* is a product of the conflict between individual and community in inegalitarian orders. According to Marx's critique of Hegel, the contradiction between individual and community is masked by an ideological figuring of the state as the representation of universality and community—a domain where harmony as well as freedom and equality can be said to prevail, and where the conflicts, unfreedoms, and inegalitarianism of civil society can be reconciled or discounted as comparatively insubstantial.

> [O]ut of this very contradiction between the interest of the individual
> and that of the community, the latter takes an independent form as
> the *State*, divorced from the real interests of individual and commu-
> nity, and at the same time as an illusory communal life, always based,
> however, on real ties existing in every family and tribal conglomera-
> tion . . . and . . . on the classes . . . which in every such mass of men
> separate out and of which one dominates all the others. . . .
>
> It follows from this that all struggles within the State . . . are merely
> the illusory forms in which the real struggles of the different classes
> are fought out among one another. (p. 160)

In casting the state as an *illusory* domain of both politics and community, Marx would seem to be figuring the state as more than simply
the vehicle of their mystification: it is also the site of their displacement or postponement. The mere presence of the state signals the absence of community and the displacement of "real struggles" among
groups to a venue that both distorts and limits those struggles, a venue
where they cannot be resolved. The state emerges in response to the
contradiction between the interest of the individual and the community, a contradiction produced by the unequal social division of labor.
Thus, some version of the state and its dissimulation of political life
come into being under any conditions of inequality. While individuals
experience their civil relations through the idiom of individualism and
conflict, capitalist relations of production situate them in interdependence. Subjects are simultaneously bound in enmity and dependency,
a contradiction smoothed ideologically by economic theories of the
hidden hand, political theories of the benefits of interest group conflict, and philosophies of utilitarianism, each of which converts com-
petitive self-interest into the common good. Marx, however, regards
this contradiction as not only inherent to capitalism but also at the
root of the ideology that presents the political sphere as the domain
of community, equality, and freedom, and at the root of the production of bourgeois individualism in civil society. The state represents
the illusion of universal representation and reconciliation of antagonistic civil interests.

In his "Critique of Hegel's Philosophy of Right" and "On the Jewish
Question," Marx argues that the state is only necessary *because* of

conflict in civil society; the state presupposes rather than abolishes or resolves that conflict. Without it, the state would have no *raison d'être*: "Far from abolishing [the] effective differences [among individuals in civil society], the state only exists so far as they are presupposed."[35] State legitimacy is rooted in the logic of ideology that reverses this presupposition, the logic that figures the state's universality as prior to rather than dependent on civil conflict. Yet this "illusion" itself generates state power and a certain form of political life, a power and a form that cannot be undone by simply puncturing the illusion on which they are based. For just as commodity fetishism and alienation cause man's own deed to become an alien power opposed to him in civil society,[36] so does the power of the state rest on the displacement (from civil society to the state) of irreconcilable conflicts in civil society. This displacement of politics, with its concomitant postponement of universalism and community, is not reversible but rather is generative of the powerful institutions of the state and the "depoliticized" character of civil society. The legitimacy of capitalism depends on its appearing as unpolitical; the legitimacy of the state depends on its appearing to have nothing to do with capitalism or other media of social conflict. Both rely on the logic of inversion constitutive of ideology in inegalitarian orders—that is, on the logic of power in ideology itself. In short, Marx's materialism ends up locating a crucial operation of power in the very realm he sought to debunk as pure mystification, mere words.

. . . .

The logic of ideology traced thus far does not conclude with the illusory form of community provided by the state in alienated civil society. Marx is also at pains to show how the relation between state and civil society mirrors, requires, and reproduces that between Christian formulations of heaven and earth, and to show why Christianity is therefore the necessary rather than historically contingent religion of the modern state. The most succinct account of this mirroring occurs in "On the Jewish Question," in a passage immediately following Marx's explanation of the fundamental mechanism of the liberal state discussed above—its presupposition of the very social powers (property, social rank, etc.) that it claims to overcome through their political abolition, its entrenchment in civil society of the particular elements that its universalism claims to transcend. On the heels of this argument, Marx writes:

> All the presuppositions of this egoistic life continue to exist in *civil society* outside the political sphere, as qualities of civil society. Where the political state has attained to its full development, man leads, not only in thought, in consciousness, but in *reality*, in *life*, a double existence—celestial and terrestrial. He lives in the *political community*, where he regards himself as a *communal being*, and in *civil society* where he acts simply as a *private* individual, treats other men as means, degrades himself to the role of a mere means, and becomes the plaything of alien powers. The political state, in relation to civil society, is just as spiritual as is heaven in relation to earth. It stands in the same opposition to civil society, and overcomes it in the same manner as religion overcomes the narrowness of the profane world, i.e., it has always to acknowledge it again, re-establish it, and allow itself to be dominated by it.[37]

Again, the question is whether the relation Marx ascribes to religion and the structure of a modern political order is homological, analogical, or causal. Does political life *realize* a certain religious formation? Is it more accurately understood as *occasioned* by that formation? In fact, Marx here surrenders the relatively simple notion of the *camera obscura*, which depicts ideology as the inversion of material reality, for a more complex and less easily metaphorized understanding of the subset of ideology that is religious consciousness. For religion does not merely invert material conditions but expresses elements of them, such as the separation of man "from himself and other men." In this vein, Marx describes political emancipation from religion (the formal secularism of the state and citizenship) as the moment at which religion ceases to be the "spirit of the state" and becomes instead "the spirit of civil society, of the sphere of egoism and of the *bellum omnium contra omnes*. It has become . . . an expression of the fact that man is *separated* from the *community*, from himself and other men."[38] Religion thus symptomatically *expresses* a certain experience, both emotional and physical in content, and so requires a reading attentive to the symptom it conveys. In Louis Althusser's formulation of this dimension of ideology in Marx, "men do indeed express, not the relation between them and their conditions of existence but *the way* they live the relation between them and their conditions of existence: this presupposes both a real relation and an 'imaginary,' 'lived' relation. . . . In ideology, the real relation is inevitably invested in the imaginary relation."[39] It is this slide between the "real" relation and "the way the relation is lived," it is the way in which the imaginary "carries" the real relation, that the notion of the *camera obscura* cannot capture, a failure that makes necessary a more complex but also less systematic formulation of the mediations entailed in ideological expression and functioning.

For Marx, religious consciousness expresses not only a particular relation to existing conditions but also, potentially, yearnings for a different order. He reads its fantastic formulations as a kind of mass utopian political theory. Just as the ideology of universality, freedom, and equality in the liberal state signifies the desire for those unrealized values, so the Christian precepts of the brotherhood of man or absolute equality before God represent the unrealized longing for true community and equality.[40] Religion and religious consciousness also represent the displacement of our own human powers onto magical or fantastic entities: "Just as Christ is the intermediary to whom man attributes all his own divinity and all his religious *bonds*, so the state is the intermediary to which man confides all his non-divinity and all his *human freedom*."[41] In the figures of the state and of Christ, ideology is shown to take very concrete forms: more than mere ideas or attachments of consciousness, ideology attributes to the *institutions* of the church and the state powers that are not their own, powers that are actually human capacities and human effects that circuitously come to be invested in church and state. But the attribution itself confers power on these institutions, thus making it at least partly true. Indeed, the power of these institutions is largely constituted by their systematic relations of misrecognition and misinvestment. From this perspective, the Althusserian construal of ideology as a force that itself produces the subject through its interpellative function appears to be far closer to Marx's own understanding than is often conceived.[42] Consider this passage from the "Jewish Question":

> But the consummation of the idealism of the state was at the same time the consummation of the materialism of civil society. . . . The *formation of the political state*, and the dissolution of civil society into independent *individuals* whose relations are regulated by *law*, . . . are accomplished by *one and the same* act. Man as a member of civil society—non-political man—necessarily appears as the natural man. . . . Egoistic man is the passive, given result of the dissolution of society.[43]

Marx here confesses the accomplishment of the state—a "celestial" and ideological entity—in dividing man against himself, in producing the depoliticization of civil society (i.e., dissolving civil society into its elements), and thus in bringing about the very political order and political subject that render ideology as power. This same confession, however, undermines the notion of power as generative only in its strictly material form. Indeed, it undermines the claim that civil society alone is the "theatre of all history."[44]

Although Marx does not make the argument himself, the state could be said to be *fetishized* much as commodities are, and to follow a similar logic of power and power's disguise. For the state, too, embodies "a definite social relation between men that assumes, in their eyes, the fantastic form of a relation between things,"[45] where the things at issue are institutions such as laws, rights, and parliaments. In this case, however, it is not human labor power but human political potential and political yearnings that are reified and refracted in state institutions. And these elements—potential and yearnings—cannot be commodified in the same way that labor can, precisely because of their intangible dimensions, their nondefinite quality. Hence Marx's alternative phraseology: referring to the state as the "intermediary between man and human liberty" and to Christ as the "intermediary to whom man attributes all his own divinity and his religious bonds," he concludes that "the state is the intermediary to which man *confides* all his non-divinity and all his *human* freedom."[46] Marx's language here— that of "attributing" and "confiding" (*verlegen*: "to transfer," in the sense of mislaying or misplacing)—is quite different from a language of exploiting, extracting, and expropriating. In attributing and confiding freedom and nondivinity to institutions and phantasms, man gives up by mislaying his capaciousness and independence, his sensual enjoyment of himself, his powers of self-governance. This disavowal or depowerment is not voluntary, of course, but is driven by orders of power (church, state, and economy) that solicit and depend on it. Regardless of how it is accomplished, however, the mislaying itself becomes a power, a political fact with enormous consequences. Like any fetish, the state becomes real and agentic through attribution, through psychic and social investment. Thus attribution is generative and not simply deflective, an admission Marx makes again and again despite his inability to fully follow its implications. Mystification tacitly emerges in his early writings not simply as a cover for power but as a source of power, a maker of history.

This brief exploration of the relation between state, ideology, religion, and civil society suggests that the model as well as the logic of power pertinent to the state and religion implicates Marx's analysis in the fetishism it criticizes. In its difference from the model of power offered in *Capital*, it also suggests the limits of the latter model for understanding the economy. Would Marx have acknowledged as much had he been able to return to the problem of the state and ideology in the unfinished part of *Capital* intended to take up these subjects? Would *Capital*, as science, have survived the return?

· · · ·

Marx's effort to contain power in a *critical mode* through a strict materialist accounting of power is undone by his own recognition that the institutions and ideas generated by particular modes of production (religion, the state, ideology) are themselves locales of power—generative, creative, capable of making history. Power that he means to contain and represent by materialist analysis—to render logical, predictable, and hydraulic—repeatedly resists such containment and representation in the course of his own labors. Power can no more be distinguished from its presentation than it can be separated from its particular institutional forms. Notwithstanding Marx's strenuous attempt to make it do so, power does not bear a constant shape nor redound to a single source. It does not follow causal—linear or dialectical—routes; it is not calculable in all of its effects; it does not remain material in substance. And it is Marx himself, in his extraordinary attunement to the workings of power, who implicitly perceives its recalcitrance, its resistance to capture by the logics he advances. Marx's effort to tame or contain power in a *normative mode*—figured in his fantasy of an order in which power's capacity for domination is completely negated by being completely shared, and in which power emerges unadorned because the need for disguise has presumably evaporated—is undone by his own recognition of power's unsharability. It is undone as well by Marx's appreciation of mystification and fetishism as themselves modalities of power.

The logics of power in Marx do not hold. When they are not patently religious, they are subtly unraveling or are exceeded by Marx's own insights into the unruly and disseminating tendencies of power. Yet these logics are clutched tightly today by those who favor a materialism that is putatively objective, logical, linear (or even multilinear), and concrete over postfoundationalist emphases on indeterminacy, contingency, unintended effects, and unsystematic emergences. What are the grounds of critique, and of normative visions, that can work free of these logics? This is, of course, the question that preoccupies critical theory today; it is one that can be answered neither by an uncritical return to Marx, nor by a return to the idealist tradition he subjected to critique, nor by a straightforward embrace of Foucaultian genealogy—the latter itself sharing some of the conceits about power's inherently logical yet hidden operation discerned in Marx. It is a question on which the future of left thinking turns, and its address requires a philosophy of history integrated into a political theory in which postfoundationalist thought is forced to yield its insights about power to normative values generated by a deliberative democratic process itself attuned to the unmasterable dimensions of power.

FIVE

■ ■ ■ ■

POLITICS

Politics without Banisters:
Genealogical Politics in Nietzsche and Foucault

> I have a metaphor . . . which I have never published but kept for myself. I call it thinking without a bannister. In German, *Denken ohne Gelander.* That is, as you go up and down the stairs you can always hold onto the bannister so that you don't fall down. But we have lost this bannister. . . .
> [In totalitarianism] those who were still very firmly convinced of the so-called old values were the first to be ready to change their old values for a new set of values, provided they were given one. And I am afraid of this, because I think that the moment you give anybody a new set of values—or this famous "bannister"—you can immediately exchange it. And the only thing the guy gets used to is having a "bannister" and a set of values, no matter. I do not believe that we can stabilize the situation in which we have been since the seventeenth century in any final way.
> —Hannah Arendt, "Hannah Arendt on Hannah Arendt"

> Convictions are more dangerous enemies of truth than lies.
> —Friedrich Nietzsche, *Human, All Too Human*

In the final months of the 1996 presidential campaign, political pundits argued that Bill Clinton's speeches reconfigured him from a president who was a policy wonk to a man of conviction.[1] For some it was a sign that he was growing into the presidency, assuming its mantle in a way that his modesty and boyishness had previously prevented. Others read it as an effort at generating the "politics of meaning" that the unholy combination of the First Lady and Michael Lerner had heralded during his first election campaign. But all agreed that conviction was also filling a space: the space of action and possibility that was eliminated by the Republican congressional sweep two years before. If it was not possible for a Democratic president to *do* much of anything, he could certainly make pronouncements about the wrongs of poverty, of crime, of broken families, and he could take unwavering stances on matters as critical to America's future as school uniforms and the V-chip in televisions. His presentation as a "man full of conviction," as the *New York Times* described him in an editorial, was precisely the measure of his impotence.

Are convictions always substitutes for action, or was the Clinton case a peculiar one? What is the relationship of conviction to politics? What is the character of each, and why do thinkers as disparate as Nietzsche, Weber, and Yeats disparage conviction, especially in political life? If not always a simple substitute for action, does conviction nonetheless resist action's historically contingent and morally unpredictable nature?

For all of its conventional association with political virtue, the *Oxford English Dictionary* reminds us that *conviction* is for the most part an unlovely word. Its meanings range from concession to a state of sinfulness, as defined by Saint Paul—"the fact or condition of being convicted or convinced of sin"—to the act of proving someone guilty of an offense or of reprehensible conduct (as in convicting a criminal), or proving someone to be in error (as in convicting an opponent in a debate). To be "under conviction," even while partaking of the secular condition of "being convinced" or having "strong belief on the ground of satisfactory reasons or evidence," also carries a religious dimension, suggested by Paul's interpretation of Jesus: "to be in the state of awakened consciousness of sin." As modern Baptists use the term, to be under conviction is to be on the road to conversion, able to hear the truth of the Lord even if one cannot yet articulate that truth: it is to be gripped by a truth that is not yet one's own to wield and speak. Like its criminal cousin, conviction of this sort signifies a condition of being pinned, trapped, unfree to act.

In contrast to conventional assumptions about conviction's relatively inert status within a moral subject, this brief consideration of its dictionary definitions suggests that to be gripped by conviction is to be in an urgent, aggressive, yet also paralyzing state. The aggression and paralysis might be confined to the closed circuit of a single subject in its cycle of sin, guilt, and reason, or they might be distributed onto other subjects. Viewed from this angle, conviction appears as a powerful tool of discursive subjection, the consummate performative speech act in which the guilt of another or the state of one's own conscience is overtly produced through aggressive argument. It may be that this particular subject formation also partakes of something distinctly modern insofar as it represents a precarious achievement that must resist rival forces (which it can never fully vanquish): counterreasons, or counterdesires. Conviction signals not only virtue's (always partial) triumph over sin, but also truth's always partial triumph over error—truth's prosecutorial relationship to error and misguidedness, and hence its uncertainty of itself in modernity. The aggression and paralysis entailed in conviction, its urgency and anxiety, remind us again that enlightenment is always bounded by encroaching dark, that in modernity truth has never really been fully convinced of itself.

In our own time, rather than providing resolution that sheds more light, conviction has come to a crisis in its presumptions: it is exposed as religious at the moment that reason is toppled as a god. If conviction is a matter of tenacious belief supported by fistfuls of reasons, then this exposure of reason leaves only tenaciousness as conviction's substance. Hence the figure of "clinging to one's convictions" comes to figure conviction itself. In this moment as well, the two meanings of conviction that appear oxymoronic in an Enlightenment frame—conviction as religious belief on the one hand, and conviction as a position supported by Reason, conviction as Truth, on the other—are rendered consistent. In collapsing into each other, both lose a certain power.

But there is really nothing to grieve here. Conviction—as Truth *or* as principle—was never the right modality for belief within a democratic polity. A politics of Truth is inevitably totalitarian, and conviction in the sense of principle converges far too easily in liberal democracies with individualist strains of moral absolutism. Thus, a politics of conviction is quite at odds with democratic deliberation. Moreover, a politics of conviction—like a politics of principle, or what Weber calls an "ethic of absolute ends"—sits uneasily in a realm whose medium is action and whose constitutive elements are therefore those of contingency, opportunity, invention, and compromise.[2] The quintessentially *political* question—the question that is both politically relevant and politically responsible—is not "What do you believe in?" but "What is to be done given a certain ensemble of political values, given a certain set of hopes or aims, and given who and where we are in history and culture?" While belief by itself takes no measure of history, context, or effect, the question of what is to be done dwells only in these elements.

I do not mean to suggest that politics cannot harbor sustained purposes; there would be little reason for valuing it if it did no more than broker the human will to power. Politics requires aims that exceed the question of power in order not to become sheer aggression, in order not to be purely self-serving, in order not to devolve into nihilistic frivolity (but don't we also know that it always flirts with each of these conditions?). Yet such political aims need not be any less historically and contextually contingent than the conditions out of which the aims are born and in which they intervene; they need not precede or transcend the political domain. Transcendent ideals in politics—convictions—are, precisely, refusals to allow history and contingency to contour the existing dimensions and possibilities of political life. In this sense, they constitute repudiations of politics, even as they masquerade as its source of redemption. Indeed, we might say that the insistence on the importance of transcendent ideals in politics paradoxically affirms rather than challenges a figuring of the political domain as relentlessly amoral. It places the idealist actor at a distance from politics, thus inevitably disappointed by it and perhaps even prepared to renounce politics because of its failures and compromises vis-à-vis his or her ideals.

This chapter considers how the notion of genealogy formulated by Nietzsche and revised by Foucault might function as an alternative ground for generating political aims—a ground that, unlike conviction, embraces the contingent elements of political life and also faces forthrightly the relative arbitrariness of political values. In the course of this consideration, I shall focus on both the deconstructive and the historical dimensions of genealogical knowledge as two crucial elements of a radical democratic politics released from conviction. Together, these dimensions enable the crafting of a theoretical frame for a historically conscious critique of the present that recurs neither to universal norms nor to conviction.

NIETZSCHE

In his polemic on behalf of genealogy, "Nietzsche, Genealogy, History," Foucault suggests that unlike other genres of philosophical or historical criticism, genealogy permits an examination of our condition that calls into question the very terms of its construction. Through its inquiry into the "past of the present," in which the categories constitutive of the present are themselves rendered historical, genealogy exposes the power of the terms by which we live; it does violence to their ordinary ordering and situation, and hence to their givenness. In thus dislocating that which is both its starting point and its object, the present, genealogy also dislocates by refiguring the terms of politics, morality, and even epistemology constitutive of the present.

Nietzsche offers a convergent, if more allegorical, recognition of genealogy's power in the preface to *On the Genealogy of Morals*. "We are unknown to ourselves, we men of knowledge," Nietzsche proclaims, because we are always circling around the "beehives of our knowledge" rather than dwelling in, and thus knowing, human experience.[3] Nietzsche's project with genealogy is to create some kind of distance between us and our knowledge, unsettling what we think we know, defamiliarizing the familiar, defamiliarizing us with ourselves. This entails, among other things, calling into question all the elements of human practices that have been attributed to a place or source outside of humanity, calling into question the a priori, and, most important, calling into question God as the source of evil. In ceasing "to look for the origin of evil behind the world" (p. 17), Nietzsche will instead discern it inside particular formations and formulations of morality, thereby disrupting both the givenness of a particular moral precept and the notion of origins as something left behind.

The genealogical work of defamiliarizing also entails asking whether values do what they claim or instead serve a purpose that must be *deciphered*. This inquiry is enabled by asking first, "under what conditions did man devise these value judgements good and evil"; second, "what value do they themselves possess"; and third, "are they a sign of distress, of impoverishment, of the degeneration of life . . . or is there revealed in them . . . the plenitude, force, and will of life." As Nietzsche describes this questioning, he also describes its productivity: "Out of my answers there grew new questions, inquiries, conjectures, probabilities—until at length I had a country of my own, a soil of my own, an entire discrete, thriving, flourishing world, like a secret garden the existence of which no one suspected" (p. 17). This secret garden is what genealogy intends to produce: this other way of conceiving the familiar, this radical displacement of the lay of the land through which we think and perceive ourselves, our problems, our imperatives. Genealogy promises a worldview that is differently populated and oriented than the one in which we are steeped. "The project is to traverse with quite novel questions, as though with new eyes, the enormous, distant, and so well hidden land of morality—of morality that has actually existed, actually been lived . . . to *discover* this land for the first time" (p. 21).

The promise of genealogy is developed in the next section of the preface, where Nietzsche outlines the explicit problem that will preoccupy him in the first essay of the text, that of conventional morality:

> This problem of the *value* of pity and of the morality of pity . . . seems at first to be merely something detached, an isolated question mark; but whoever sticks with it and *learns* how to ask questions here will experience what I experienced—a tremendous new prospect opens up for him, a new possibility comes over him like a vertigo, every kind of mistrust, suspicion, fear leaps up, his belief in morality, in all morality, falters—finally a new demand becomes audible. (p. 20)

Nietzsche here suggests that genealogy is a form of artful questioning, a way of asking "what really happened there" about a commonplace. But this questioning inevitably disturbs a much larger nest of beliefs than the one with which the genealogist begins. Recall the projects of Nietzsche's *Genealogy of Morals*, of Foucault's *History of Sexuality* or *Discipline and Punish*, and the way in which each interrogates not only certain conventional beliefs and histories but also their structure and function in a larger social project. Each begins with a story by which we commonly "know" ourselves—as morally good, enlightened, sexually liberated, politically humane—and queries both whether these stories are "really true" and what function of power each purported truth serves, what each fiction disguises, displaces, enforces, and mobilizes. Each study also opens out well beyond its initial question to consider the imbrications in modernity of power, subject formation, conscience, guilt, confession, and more. The vertigo that genealogy aims to achieve means that more than a particular subject of knowledge is transformed by the genealogical inquiry; the knower, too, is cast into unfamiliarity with her- or himself. The genealogist will experience—psychologically and physiologically as well as epistemologically—a loss of ground, as particular narratives and presumptions are upended and scrutinized for the interests they serve and the comfort they offer.

The questioning that Nietzsche specifies as being able to achieve this effect is of a specific historical kind:

> Let us articulate this new demand [that has become audible by virtue of questioning the value of the morality of pity]: we need a critique of moral values, the value of these values themselves must first be called in question—and for that there is needed a *knowledge of the conditions and circumstances in which they grew, under which they evolved and changed, a knowledge of a kind that has never yet existed or even been desired*. (p. 20, emphasis added)

Calling into question a commonplace (in this case, the value of the morality of pity) produces a new political-theoretical demand (a critique of morality as such), that in turn produces a need for a new kind of knowledge (a particular kind of history of morality). To engage in a political critique of values, to question the value of certain values, one must know the conditions under which they emerged, changed, and took hold, how they converged with or displaced other values, what their emergence fought off, valorized, and served. This is the history that is buried by the naturalization of values as universal and transhistorical. This is also the history that conviction operates *within* and hence cannot articulate, let alone challenge.

There is something else to note in the passage just cited. The movement it tracks between knowledge and politics, between questioning and demand, consists of an oscillation that does not collapse these terms into one another: questioning produces an experience of vertigo, and the vertigo gives way to a demand. The demand is not of a conventional political sort but rather seeks new knowledge—vertiginous knowledge when developed and practiced within the culture it aims to unravel. The questioning, the vertigo, the demand, the knowledge, and the political dislocation all incite one another, but the chain of incitation would be aborted if the movement collapsed either through the direct politicization of knowledge or through the reduction of politics to questioning, to pure critique.

In the next passage of the preface, Nietzsche introduces genealogy's strategy of reversal:

> One has taken the value of these "values" as given, as factual, as beyond all question; one has hitherto never doubted or hesitated in the slightest degree in supposing "the good man" to be of greater value than "the evil man," of greater value in the sense of furthering the advancement and prosperity of man in general. . . . But what if the reverse were true? What if a symptom of regression were inherent in the "good," likewise a danger, a seduction, a poison, a narcotic, through which the present was possibly living at the expense of the future? So that precisely morality was the danger of dangers? (p. 20)

We can here see three different instances of genealogy's strategy of reversal. First, Nietzsche challenges everyday values assumed to be unchallengeable, thereby reversing their givenness in an effort to disclose the power this givenness carries and covers. Whatever has been accepted "as factual, as beyond all question," will now be considered dubious, as a possible fiction. Second, while reversals function as a form of questioning, they also emerge as a hypothetical response to those questions: the morally good is hypostasized as dangerous, the opposite of its conventional self-representation. Finally, genealogy also conjures a reversal in the course of history—it challenges progressive accounts with intimations of regression, as it suggests that the present may be "living at the expense of the future" rather than paving the way to that future.

Each of these reversals is important in Foucault's appropriation of genealogy, to which we next turn. Equally important to Foucault is Nietzsche's emphasis on tracking historical emergences in terms of the interests they serve (rather than the benefits they confer), as well as Nietzsche's belief that it is "democratic prejudice in the modern world toward all questions of origin" that prevents us from being able to see these powers and interests clearly (p. 28). But though Foucault draws extensively from Nietzsche, he eliminates from genealogical work the constitutive place Nietzsche assigned to desire and ideals, and especially to their interplay in forming historically specific subjects and in crafting history. Yet Nietzsche's "psychology," which Foucault jettisons, is fundamental rather than incidental to Nietzsche's genealogy: desire not only animates history but is transformed by it. If genealogy traces, *inter alia*, the historical variability of human beings themselves, our changing form and content as historical subjects, then desire is both the source of this plasticity and the surface on which it unfolds.

For Foucault, it is not the will to power in desire but power more broadly and diffusely conceived that moves human history and transforms human subjects. Not desire and ideals but social power and its cousin, knowledge, make up the terms of genealogical inquiry. Indeed, Foucault could be seen as offering a (non-Marxist) materialist corrective to Nietzsche's idealist account of the history of the subject. While Foucault's subject is no more constant than Nietzsche's, it is power rather than the codification of transmogrifications of desire into ideals that transforms the positioning and subjectivity of the Foucaultian subject; it is power that gives shape to values, that generates certain kinds of knowledge ambitions and hegemonic knowledges. Desires, values, and cultural ideals are not sources but effects of power. In turning from Nietzsche to Foucault, then, we see genealogy not merely developed but transformed, as we move from its formulation by an avowedly anti-political and expressly psychological thinker for whom genealogy served to subvert the pieties of moral philosophy to its reworking by a political and relatively anti-psychological thinker for whom genealogy cuts against the grain of progressive political shibboleths.

FOUCAULT

In "Nietzsche, Genealogy, History," his most sustained discussion of genealogy, Foucault does not say what genealogy is but what it defines itself against, what conventions of history and metaphysics it aims to disrupt. This markedly *indirect* articulation of genealogy itself exemplifies the practice of genealogy. "Nietzsche, Genealogy, History" is an account of contemporary values—in particular, progressive history and metaphysical critique—as problematic fictions; it is an alternative story of our commonplaces that aims to reveal their fictive and hence fragile character. It is a production that reveals the terms by which we live through rupturing them, through doing violence to their ordinary ordering and situation. Foucault's account of genealogy here also mirrors genealogical practice in its emergence through conflict and through its tracing of forces—not groups, individuals, or concepts—in battle. Foucault eschews any attempt to explain genealogy by systematically articulating a coherent method it might entail, and depicts it instead as an embattled "emergence"—something that must fight for place and, more specifically, must displace other conventions of history in order to prevail.

For Foucault, genealogy emerges in opposition to progressive historiography on one side and to metaphysics on the other. Yet it also tenders a genealogical critique of what it opposes insofar as it reveals how each of these practices is implicated in the other: the emergence of genealogy exposes the metaphysics in progressive historiography and the unself-conscious historical framing of any metaphysics. This exposure in turn serves the positive task of developing a philosophically self-conscious historiography (a historiography loosened from or at least capable of avowing the historically specific metanarratives it invokes) and a historically self-conscious philosophy, both of which contribute to the refiguring of political space that Foucault aims to achieve with genealogy. To see the grounds for this positive turn, we must first examine in closer detail the negative program of genealogy—the fundamentalisms it seeks to disrupt, the denaturalizations it strives to perform.

. . . .

> The genealogist needs history to dispel the chimeras of the origin, somewhat in the manner of the pious philosopher who needs a doctor to exorcise the shadow of his soul.
> —Michel Foucault, "Nietzsche, Genealogy, History"

Genealogy, according to Foucault's reading of Nietzsche, is not to be confused with a quest for origins; yet it will not "neglect as inaccessible the vicissitudes of history" and altogether eschew the problem of what Foucault significantly renames as "beginnings." Rather, genealogy will "cultivate the details and accidents that accompany every beginning; it will be scrupulously attentive to their petty malice . . . await their emergence . . . not be reticent in 'excavating the depths.' "[4] Foucault contrasts the genealogical emphasis on beginnings as a field of accident, disparity, conflict, and haphazardness with conventional history's pure or "distant ideality of the [idea of] origin." The former is temporally imprecise, unevenly and porously bounded in space, and directionally without aim; the latter fantasizes a purposive and characteristically teleological event or formation. Similarly, history as a "concrete body of a development" is contrasted with a notion of history as the travels of pure soul; genealogy is crucially materialist, albeit in a non-Marxist and even noneconomic idiom.

While genealogy metaphorizes history as body—"with its moments of intensity, its lapses, its extended periods of feverish agitation, its fainting spells"—genealogy also treats the body itself as relentlessly historical. The body is "the inscribed surface of events" as well as "a volume in perpetual disintegration" (p. 83). But neither the corporeality of history nor the historicity of the body can be brought into relief without challenging the purity of origins and attendant notions of progressive development—it is the presumed constancy of the body and the presumed conceptual motion of history that secure the purity of origins. Similarly, neither the extent to which history is composed of feelings, sentiments, and power nor the historicity of feelings, sentiments, and power—their nonessential and mutable character—can be discerned until that composition and historicity are grasped as mutually constitutive, until the suprahistorical perspective that denies them a place in history is supplanted by genealogical analysis. Thus, what Foucault sometimes calls "effective history" or genealogy "differs from traditional history in being without constants" (p. 87). Fredric Jameson's maxim, "always historicize," appears relatively modest next to Foucault's ambition for genealogy, which might be summed up, *historicize everything*. But what kind of historicization?

. . . .

> Genealogy does not resemble the evolution of a species and
> does not map the destiny of a people.
> —Michel Foucault, "Nietzsche, Genealogy, History"

As the study of "stock" or "descent" rather than development, as that which reverses the direction in which historians conventionally proceed (tracing the past of the present rather than searching for the present in the past), genealogy invites "the dissociation of the self, its recognition and displacement as an empty synthesis" (p. 81). As it inverts conventional historical vision to regard historical scenes of conflicts and accidents as contingently constitutive of the present, genealogy seeks to deconstruct essentialist and every other stable notion of the body and the self; it disrupts coherent identities, both individual and collective. Foucault's emphasis on "accidents," "errors," and "faulty calculations" as that which "gave birth to those things that continue to exist and have value for us" aims to replace the notion that "truth or being [lies] at the root of what we know or what we are" (p. 81) with an appreciation of the contingent—not merely accidental but noninevitable—features of our existence. If everything about us is the effect of historical accident rather than will or design, then we are, paradoxically, both more severely historical and also more plastic than we might otherwise seem. We are more sedimented by history, but also more capable of intervening in our histories, than is conceivable through historiographies that preserve some elements of humans and of time as fixed in nature. "Nothing in man," Foucault writes, "is sufficiently stable to serve as the basis for . . . understanding other men" (p. 87).

One of the most important aims of genealogy is to denaturalize existing forces and formations more thoroughly than either conventional history or metaphysical criticism can do—to take that which appears to be given and provide it not simply a history but one that reveals how contingently it came into being and remains in being, the degree to which it is neither foreordained nor fixed in meaning. This kind of history is precisely the opposite of teleological history; indeed, it is in a permanent quarrel with teleological history, insofar as it treats the present as the accidental production of the contingent past, rather than treating the past as the sure and necessary road to the inevitable present. Moreover, the heritage traced by genealogy is neither an "acquisition" nor a "possession that grows and solidifies" but "an unstable assemblage of faults, fissures, and heterogeneous layers that threaten the fragile inheritor from within or from underneath" (p. 82). This formulation, too, by supplanting an evolutionary with a geological image, metaphorically recasts the weight of history as something that works not through linearity or pure temporality, not as a force or a thing moving through time, but through spatial accretion—"heterogeneous layers." This weight results in part from the paradoxical fact that the genealogist treats time more gravely—is more attentive to its power as a field of forces in space—than does the historian guided by a suprahistorical perspective that "finds its support outside of time" (p. 87). Yet again, even as history's weight is multiplied by this perspective, so also are its inconsistency and contingency brought into relief: "the search for descent . . . disturbs what was previously considered immobile; it fragments what was thought unified; it shows the heterogeneity of what was imagined consistent with itself" (p. 87). The "things" of history decompose under the genealogist's scrutiny.

Through these transformations in both the objects and movement of history, genealogy reorients the relationship of history to political possibility: although the present field of political possibility is constrained by its histories, those histories are themselves tales of improbable, uneven, and unsystematic emergence, and thus contain openings for disturbance. In place of the lines of determination laid down by laws of history, genealogy appears as a field of openings—faults, fractures, and fissures. Conversely, rather than promising a certain future, as progressive history does, genealogy only opens possibilities through which various futures might be pursued. Openings along fault lines and incitements from destabilized (because denaturalized) configurations of the present form the stage of political possibility. But these openings and incitements dictate neither the terms nor the direction of political possibility, both of which are matters of imagination and invention (themselves limited by what Foucault terms the "political ontology of the present").

. . . .

> As it is wrong to search for descent in an uninterrupted continuity, we should avoid thinking of emergence as the final term of a historical development.
> —Michel Foucault, "Nietzsche, Genealogy, History"

Just as histories of emergent phenomena or formations are tales of conflicts, convergences, and accidents, so these phenomena or formations are cast by genealogy as "episodes" rather than "culminations." The metaphysics of conventional histories, in placing present needs at the origin, fail to grasp the subjugating forces that constitute the dynamic of history; they substitute "the anticipatory power of meaning" for "the hazardous play of dominations" (p. 83). Genealogy promises dirty histories, histories of power and subjection, histories of bids for hegemony waged, won, or vanquished—the "endlessly repeated play of dominations" (p. 85) rather than histories of reason, meaning, or higher purposes. Genealogy traces continual yet discontinuous histories, histories without direction yet also without end, histories of varied and protean orders of subjection. "Humanity does not gradually progress from combat to combat until it arrives at universal reciprocity[;] . . . humanity installs each of its violences in a system of rules and thus proceeds from domination to domination" (p. 85). The content, the lived modality, of "effective history" is politics, and the moving force of this history is an often diffused, sometimes institutionalized, sometimes sublimated will to power. Put the other way around, there are no nonpolitical moments in genealogical history. With genealogy, we can no longer speak of an "engine" of history, because genealogy makes clear that history is not propelled; it does not lead forward but is rather the retrospective record of conflicts that yield an emergence. History is no longer "moved" because it does not harbor direction, ends, or end, even while it bears generative processes.[5] "[N]o one is responsible for an emergence; no one can glory in it since it always occurs in the interstice" (p. 85).

The space of this kind of dirty history is what Nietzsche and Foucault both call a non-place, a "pure distance," a "place of confrontation" (p. 85). It is a non-place because in the confrontation or battle that genealogy seeks to document, at the site of emergence, contestants do not oppose each other within an order that houses them both; instead, each fights to bring into being an order (Foucault sometimes recurs to the infelicitous language of "system") in their respective images. The "place" that will feature the constituents recognized by the historian does not exist until the contest has been (provisionally) won; the contestants do not acquire their identities until the battle is (provisionally) over; the elements in a new regime do not exist until that regime has (provisionally) emerged, until a new order of meaning and power has been brought into being. Genealogy refuses to feature individuals, parties, or even purposes as straightforwardly agentic or accountable in modernist terms, because Foucault appreciates the extent to which the entity that would be held accountable by conventional ethics does not yet exist when such ethics is demanding that it justify itself and its actions. Thus, instead of featuring parties to a battle, genealogy documents "the entry of forces[,] . . . their eruption, the leap from the wings to center stage" (p. 84). Moreover, these forces themselves change over time: "the isolation of different points of emergence does not conform to the successive configurations of an identical meaning." The effort to disrupt a narrative that essentializes historical forces includes documenting "substitutions, displacements, disguised conquests, and systematic reversals." Only then can a metaphysics committed to the "slow exposure of the meaning hidden in an origin" be supplanted with an understanding that eschews a suprahistorical perspective (p. 86). And only through such an understanding can a politics animated by the moral accountability of persons for political conditions be replaced by an *effective politics*: a politics of projects and strategies rather than moral righteousness; a politics of bids for power rather than remonstrances of it.

. . . .

> History becomes "effective" to the degree that it introduces discontinuity into our very being—as it divides our emotions, dramatizes our instincts, multiplies our body and sets it against itself. "Effective" history deprives the self of the reassuring stability of life and nature, and it will not permit itself to be transported by a voiceless obstinacy toward a millennial ending.
> —Michel Foucault, "Nietzsche, Genealogy, History"

The measure of genealogy's success is its disruption of conventional accounts of ourselves—our sentiments, bodies, origins, futures. It tells a story that disturbs our habits of self-recognition, posing an "us" that is foreign. Genealogy achieves its disruptions both by disturbing popular narratives and microcosmically. Where there is narrative logic or continuity, genealogy assaults it by introducing counterforces and revelations of discontinuity: an "event" is deconstructed as "the reversal of the relationship of forces"; "destiny" is upset by insistence on "the singular randomness of events"; "profound intentions and immutable necessities" are forced into relationship with "countless lost events, without a landmark or a point of reference"; reason is revealed as a rhetorical strategy, neutral (scientific) knowledge is exposed as a massive exercise in power, and the unique individual is rewritten as a messy historical production (pp. 88–89).

 But is genealogy only perverse in its disruptions and confabulations? Does it only negate? Knowledge is "made for cutting," Foucault insists, and the political landscape dissected by genealogical knowledge is the monolith of the present, a landscape that genealogy converts into questions: What are the characteristics of power in the time in which we live? What kind of subjects has this time made of us? Or in Foucault's own phrase, "What is happening today? What is happening now? And what is this 'now' within which all of us find ourselves [do we?]; and who defines the moment at which I am writing?"

These questions, Foucault insists, cannot be answered through conventional historical or philosophical approaches.

> This is not an analytics of truth; it will concern what might be called an ontology of the present, an ontology of ourselves, and it seems to me that the philosophical choice confronting us today is this: one may opt for a critical philosophy that will present itself as an analytic philosophy of truth in general or one may opt for a critical thought that will take the form of an ontology of ourselves, an ontology of the present; it is this form of philosophy that, from Hegel, through Nietzsche and Max Weber, to the Frankfurt School, has founded a form of reflection in which I have tried to work.[6]

Now, what does Foucault mean by the odd philosophical-historical locution "ontology of the present"? He credits Kant both with this formulation of the task of philosophy and with its opposite, the development of "an analytics of truth."[7] Against the metaphysical reach of the latter, an ontology of the present asks, "What is our present? What is the present field of possible experiences?" These are the questions Foucault understands Kant to have posed about the Enlightenment, not by defining the elements of the age but by recognizing the elements of its coming into being, the struggles and partial successes of its emergence.[8] Foucault elaborates:

> I wonder if one of the great roles of philosophical thought since the Kantian '*Was ist Aufklärung?*' might not be characterized by saying that the task of philosophy is to describe the nature of the present, and of 'ourselves in the present.' . . . [T]he function of any diagnosis concerning the nature of the present . . . does not consist in a simple characterization of what we are but, instead—by following lines of fragility in the present—in managing to grasp why and how that-which-is might no longer be that-which-is. In this sense, any description must always be made in accordance with these kinds of virtual fracture which open up the space of freedom understood as a space of concrete freedom, i.e., of possible transformation.[9]

In his easy substitution of the terms *ontology, describing the nature of the present,* and *diagnosis,* Foucault hints at the function and contours of an ontology of the present. Its point would be to grasp our-

selves as "ill" in some way that exceeds the symptom without pretending to an objective standpoint and without subscribing to notions
of root or foundational causes. The goal is an understanding of the
historical composition of our being. An appreciation of the capacity
of history to produce *ontoi*, an insistence that history *and* man lack
constants, makes it possible to grasp at least partially the constituent
elements of our time, to grasp the constitutive conditions of ourselves.
Thus, while the notion of ontology points toward a certain objectivism, that objectivism is immediately undercut by the nontotalizing historical strategy through which this ontology is achieved; it seeks suffi-
cient appreciation of the fractured and contingent historicity of the
present to deprive the present of its givenness and inevitability. What
is never claimed by Foucault, what could not be claimed, is that this
historicity is exhaustive or even that the aim of genealogy—an ontology of the present—can be fully realized. The aspiration always remains an aspiration. Moreover, the grasp of the "now" and of "ourselves" that we desire will itself be motivated by something in the
present; there is no illusion that we stand apart from ourselves even
as we make an effort to part with ourselves.

Foucault's desire for a "diagnosis" or "ontology" of the present
reconfigures the relationship of philosophy to history and the relation
of philosophy and history to politics. The task of philosophy becomes
curiously historical: in apprehending the nature of ourselves in the
present, philosophy comes to recognize us as historical beings and our
time as a time in history. Conversely, history is subjected to philosophical critique insofar as it must be divested of reason and direction at
the same time as it is tethered to a conventionally philosophical question: "how can we know our time and ourselves when we cannot move
beyond or outside of them?" In "Nietzsche, Genealogy, History," Foucault describes genealogy's framing of this problem: "Effective history
studies what is closest, but in an abrupt dispossession, so as to seize it
at a distance" (p. 89). Since even genealogical "histories" are inevitably inflected with norms and aims, philosophical self-consciousness is
required so that we may attempt to track those inflections. But genealogy also requires philosophy to call into question the terms of its object of study, even as philosophy requires genealogy—the radical his-

toricization of its terms—to do the same. "Effective history," Foucault reminds us, "differs from traditional history in being without constants." It "emphatically excludes the 'rediscovery of ourselves' " and "becomes 'effective' to the degree that it introduces discontinuity into our very being" (pp. 87, 88). History bound to the task of creating an ontology of the present is thus consonant with the Socratic charge to philosophy to expose the familiar as an illness: "its task is to become a curative science" (p. 90).

In its strange mixture of genres, genealogy's effort to produce an "ontology of the present" effectively *crosses* philosophy and history, undercutting the premises by which each ordinarily excludes the other from its self-definition. At the same time, in posing the diagnostic question "who are we?" genealogy attaches both history and philosophy to a political task—that of knowing who we are, knowing our ill body and bodies. Thus, for example, in his own genealogy of contemporary "governmentality," Foucault traces the unlikely imbrication of "pastoral power" and *raison d'état* to bring into view the contemporary political rationality that not only rules but produces us: "Our civilization has developed the most complex system of knowledge, the most sophisticated structures of power: what has this kind of knowledge, this type of power made of us?"[10] Here, the notion of subjects produced by historically and culturally specific configurations of knowledge and power confounds the boundaries conventionally drawn between philosophy and history.

It is important, however, that while genealogy is concerned with the apprehension of political conditions, it does not thereby politicize intellectual inquiry. Rather, genealogy's refiguring of philosophy and history extends to a refiguring of *the political* that directly opposes this term to conventional understandings of politicization on one side and policy on the other.[11] Though genealogy may be saturated with political interests, though it is deployed to replace "laws of history" with exposures of mechanisms of power and relations of force, though it is carried out in the name of denaturalizing the present in order to highlight its malleability, genealogy neither prescribes political positions nor specifies desirable futures. Rather, it aims to make visible why particular positions and visions of the future occur to us, and especially to reveal when and where those positions work in the same register of "political rationality" as that which they purport to criticize.

Foucault pejoratively links "politicization" with "totalization" and contrasts the openness of his own genealogical studies with totalizing intellectual and political closures. This does not mean that he opposes politics as such, nor that he naively believes his intellectual endeavors to be independent of politics. Rather, he intends his inquiry to call into question certain political truths and commitments:

> I have especially wanted to question politics, and to bring to light in the political field, as in the field of historical and philosophical interrogation, some problems that had not been recognized there before. I mean that the questions I am trying to ask are not determined by a preestablished political outlook and do not tend toward the realization of some definite political project.
>
> This is doubtless what people mean when they reproach me for not presenting an overall theory. But I believe precisely that the forms of totalization offered by politics are always, in fact, very limited. I am attempting, to the contrary, apart from any *totalization*—which would be at once *abstract* and *limiting*—to *open up* problems that are as *concrete* and *general* as possible, problems that approach politics from behind and cut across societies on the diagonal.[12]

While Foucault invests genealogy with the possibility of emancipating intellectual inquiry from certain kinds of position taking and deploys it to question certain conventional left positions (e.g., those drawn from Marxism, Maoism, social democracy, or liberation politics bound to social identity), he is equally concerned to separate such inquiry from policy concerns. In his genealogy of "pastoral power," Foucault provocatively links policy with policing (and policy studies with the aims of a police state) through a study of the emergence of *Polizeiwissenschaft*, a term connoting both policy science and police science.[13] Through this genealogy, Foucault casts the very preoccupation with policy—formulating it, influencing it, studying it—less as a limitation of reformist politics (the conventional left critique) than as a symptom of a contemporary political rationality that renders quite normal the state administration of everyday life. Foucault's genealogy of the political rationality that fuses *Polizeiwissenschaft* with *raison d'état* shows how, in Colin Gordon's words, "reason of state's problem of calculating detailed actions appropriate to an infinity of . . . contingent circumstances is met by the creation of an exhaustively detailed knowledge of the governed reality of the state itself, extending (at least in aspiration) to touch the existences of its individual members. The police state is also termed the 'state of prosperity.' The idea of prosperity or happiness is the principle which identifies the state with its subjects."[14] Thus, the proliferation of policies that "constitutes a kind of omnivorous espousal of governed reality, the sensorium of a Leviathan," is intricately linked to the tacitly but ubiquitously policed order that characterizes both disciplinary society and a society saturated with policy.[15] Indeed, disciplinary society *is* the policy-bound society; it is one with the public policy state. According to Foucault, "what [the seventeenth- and eighteenth-century authors of *Polizeiwissenschaft*] . . . understand by 'police' isn't an institution or mechanism functioning within the state, but a governmental technology peculiar to the state; domains, techniques, targets where the state intervenes."[16] These interventions deal with everything concerning "life"—health, highways, public safety, workplaces, poverty—in short, all that today traffics under the rubric of "public policy." He elaborates, "The *police* includes everything. But from an extremely particular point of view. Men and things are envisioned as to their relationships: men's coexistence on a territory; their relationships as to property; what they produce; what is exchanged on the market. It also considers how they live, the diseases and accidents which can befall them. What the police sees to is a live, active, productive man."[17]

A political-intellectual focus on influencing policy would appear to further subject intellectual life to the political rationality inclusive of *Polizeiwissenschaft*, indeed abetting this rationality with the very instrument—intellectual critique—that could be used to "cut" it ("knowledge is made for cutting . . ."). Thus Foucault's turn away from a concern with policy recommendations, or from using intellectual inquiry to effect policy reform, is not simply a matter of intellectual indifference or of radical disdain for political reformism. Rather, this turn can be explained by the normative motivation for genealogy as well as by the specific genealogy of governmentality proffered in his lectures "Politics and Reason" and "Governmentality." The point of genealogy is to map the discourses and political rationalities constitutive of our time such that they are brought into relief as historical, contingent, partial, and thus malleable, such that "that-which-is" can be thought as "that-which-might-not-be." Its point is to introduce the possibility of a different discursive understanding of ourselves and our possibilities.

. . . .

Thus far I have suggested that Foucault's reformulation of the political, tendered in opposition to politicization on the one hand and to policy on the other, is the effect of genealogy's displacements of conventions of history and philosophy, especially the displacement of their conventional disidentification with one another. Against what he argues the political is not, we may now consider in closer detail three aspects of Foucault's reformulation of the political as it is inflected by genealogy: the emphasis on fracture, the emphasis on political rationality, and the sundering of genealogical discoveries from political prescription through the refutation of logics of history.

Fracture

Genealogy, Foucault argues, reveals the present to be the consequence of a history fraught with accidents, haphazard conflicts, and unrelated events that are themselves singularly random and nothing more than "the reversal of a relationship of forces."[18] Notwithstanding frequent misreadings of Foucault's thought on this point, the randomness and discontinuity of history make the past *and* present more, rather than less, difficult to understand, as they weight the present more heavily with an infinitely complex history, a history that conforms neither to temporal nor spatial logics. "The world we know is not this ultimately simple configuration where events are reduced to accentuate their essential traits, their final meaning, or their initial and final value. On the contrary, it is a profusion of entangled events." Foucault continues, quoting Nietzsche: "If it appears as a 'marvelous motley, profound and totally meaningful,' this is because it began and continues its secret existence through a 'host of errors and phantasms.'

We want historians to confirm our belief that the present rests upon profound intentions and immutable necessities. But the true historical sense confirms our existence among countless lost events, without a landmark or a point of reference."[19]

That history is composed by accidents and unrelated events is significant for political thinking because the apparent totality of the present is subjected to this nonlinear, discontinuous history, a subjection which thereby breaks apart the present. In this way, genealogy articulates politically exploitable fissures and fractures in the present; it produces openings and interstices as sites of political agitation or alternatives. Genealogy thus *reduces the political need for progressive history* as the only source of movement away from the present even as it eliminates the grounds for such history. Similarly, genealogy *reduces the political need for total revolution* even as it eliminates the possibility of such revolution by depriving the present of the status of a seamless totality, revolution's critical object. Hence Foucault's insistence that the question about the nature of our present does not consist in "a simple characterization of what we are," but rather "follows lines of fragility in the present." Fractures in history become the material of possibility in the present to the extent that they signify weaknesses or openings in the structure of the present—"virtual fracture[s] . . . open up the space of freedom."[20]

For Foucault, the project of making the present appear as something that might not be as it is constitutes *the* distinctive contribution of intellectual work to political life. It should now be clear why genealogy—which aims to reveal the wholly constructed character of the present even as it reveals discontinuities and fissures in that construction—rather than polemic or general critique, is the venue of this offering.[21] Put another way, Foucault's oft-rehearsed argument on behalf of the "specific" rather than "universal" intellectual appears now as an argument rooted in the singular powers of genealogy to bring into relief critical dimensions of the present. His jettisoning of metaphysical critique in favor of local genealogical criticism thus seems a reaction less to the dominations that metaphysical critique reiterates than to the distance that such critique fails to achieve from the constitutive terms of its own time. Recall that for Foucault, political efficacy is "not a matter of emancipating truth from every system of power (which would be a chimera . . .) but of *detaching the power of truth from the forms of hegemony*, social, economic and cultural, within which it operates at the present time."[22]

Political Rationality

This term in Foucault's work is related to what he named in his early work "episteme" and in his later work "discourse," yet it also functions differently from both. *Rationality*, as Foucault reworks it from Weber, designates the legitimating structure of any government; governmental rationality is precisely that which releases governments from the need to use physical violence. Thus, political rationality does not, as for Weber, legitimize or "cover" physical violence, but instead replaces it as a mode of governance: rationality *is* itself a modality of power. "The government of men by men . . . involves a certain type of rationality. It doesn't involve instrumental violence."[23] As we saw above in the discussion of *Polizeiwissenschaft*, "policing" itself—conventionally understood as an instance of explicit state violence—is reconfigured by Foucault as a mode of rationality. *Polizeiwissenschaft* involves detailed application of detailed knowledge to specific relationships, and its character is quite unlike the brute threat of a nightstick.

It is because Foucault opposes rationality and power to force and violence that he speaks of rationality rather than rationalization, of governmentality rather than government: "The main problem when people try to rationalize something is not to investigate whether or not they conform to principles of rationality, but to discover which kind of rationality they are using." Thus, "the criticism of power wielded over the mentally sick or mad cannot be restricted to psychiatric institutions; nor can those questioning the power to punish be content with denouncing prisons as total institutions. The question is: how are such relations of power rationalized?"[24]

While Foucault sometimes uses *political rationality* to refer to the discursive logics legitimating all regimes of power, from asylums to schools to monarchies, he also uses the term to specify a particular form of government prevailing in the modern West that "first took its stand on the idea of pastoral power, then on . . . reason of state."[25] In this second and more interesting usage, political rationality names the unique political form that yields the simultaneous processes of individualization and totalization, thereby giving rise to Foucault's signature critique of modernity. This political form has its roots in the imbrication of emerging state power with pastoral power: "If the state is the political form of a centralized and centralizing power, let us call pastorship the individualizing power."[26] Foucault does not mean to suggest that the individualizing and totalizing techniques making up modern state power were easily woven together. His genealogy of modern political power is instead intended in part to show the initially antagonistic relationship between the evolution of the state's centralizing powers and "the development of power techniques oriented towards individuals and intended to rule them in a continuous and permanent way." *Political rationality* marks the consolidation of this antagonism into the governmental form of the policing or policy state: "Just to look at nascent state rationality, just to see what its first policing project was, makes it clear that, right from the start, the state is both individualizing and totalitarian."[27]

Regardless of whether Foucault is invoking political rationality as a proper or improper noun, the invocation calls attention to the limited efficacy of any resistance or critique that attacks only the effects of a particular rationality rather than the scheme as a whole. In this regard, political rationality may be seen as replacing the notion of "the system" in political thinking, a notion that seeks to reach beyond epiphenomenal injustices in order to criticize the grounds of those injustices: "Those who resist or rebel against a form of power cannot merely be content to denounce violence or criticize an institution. Nor is it enough to cast the blame on reason in general. What has to be questioned is the form of rationality at stake. . . . Liberation can only come from attacking . . . political rationality's very roots."[28] It is precisely the difference between a "rationality" and a "system" that is significant in Foucault's reformulation of the political and that prevents this seemingly foundational account from being so. For unlike the coherently bounded, internally consistent (or internally contradictory), and relatively ahistorical figure of a system, a political rationality cannot be apprehended through empirical description or abstract principles, nor can it be falsified through general critique. Political rationalities are orders of practice and orders of discourse, not systems of rule;

what must be captured for them to be subject to political criticism is their composition as well as their contingent nature. Similarly, the exploitable weaknesses in a political rationality are not systemic contradictions; they are instead effects of fragmented histories, colliding discourses, forces that persisted without triumphing decisively, unintended effects, and arguments insecure about themselves. Such weaknesses cannot be exploited through philosophical critique that remains internal to or unaware of the terms of a particular rationality. Genealogical critique aims to reveal various rationalities as the ones in which we live, to articulate them *as* particular forms of rationality. This articulation enables us to call into question the terms of political analysis from a standpoint outside those terms as well as to discern the historically produced fissures in their construction. Hence Foucault's remark that "the history of various forms of rationality is sometimes more effective in unsettling our certitudes and dogmatism than is abstract criticism."[29]

Sundering Genealogical Discoveries from Political Prescription

Where modernist conventions of radical political critique are oriented toward systems and their contradictions, Foucault argues for articulating the political rationalities constitutive of the present. Similarly, where modernist conventions of radical political normativity consult history either to find images of alternatives to the present (what Foucault disparagingly terms "a history of solutions") or to discern "laws of history" that determine the present and future, Foucault argues for discerning political possibility—"the space of freedom"—in "lines of fragility in the present." In refusing totalizing logics to history and political life; in replacing logics of history with notions of accident, battle, and inadvertent convergence; and in replacing a notion of political systems with political rationalities, Foucault refigures how the history of the present, the nature of the present, and political possibilities in the present are related. History is figured less as a stream linking past and future than as a cluttered and dynamic field of eruptions, forces, emergences, and partial formations. As the discontinuities and lack of directional laws in history are pushed to the foreground, history is spatialized—conceptually wrenched from temporal ordering—and the political possibilities of the present are thereby expanded.

In his effort to (re)locate power in space rather than time, Foucault both highlights space as the domain of battle and brings into focus the organization of space as itself a technique of power—the Panopticon is his best-known example. Put another way, Foucault seeks to interrupt analyses of the transformations of discourse that occur in the vocabulary of time (and their invariable anthropomorphizing of history according to a model of individual human development) with a *geography* of power.[30] "Anyone envisaging the analysis of discourses solely in terms of temporal continuity would inevitably be led to approach and analyse it like the internal transformation of an individual consciousness. Which would lead to his erecting a great collective consciousness as the scene of events."[31] In a historiography bound to temporal continuity or purpose, time itself becomes a prime mover. By contrast, "to trace the forms of implantation, delimitation, and demarcation of objects, the modes of tabulation, the organisation of domains mean[s] throwing into relief . . . processes—historical ones, needless to say, of power. The spatialising description of discursive realities gives on to the analysis of related effects of power."[32]

What becomes clear here is that Foucault's "ontology of the present" is not merely a different way of casting the historical conditions that frame contemporary practices but a different way of casting those conditions as the stage for potential political invention and intervention. If history does not have a course, then it does not prescribe the future; the "weight" and contours of history establish constraints but not norms for political action. Genealogy's "designation or description of the real never has a prescriptive value of the kind, 'because this is, that will be.' "[33] If history is without a forward-moving logic, then it bears no logical entailments for the future; no inference can be drawn from it about what is to be done or what is to be valued. As history is emancipated from metaphysics and thereby becomes radically desacralized, so too politics becomes a matter of opportunity, limits, and judgment rather than unfolding historical schemes and transcendent ideals. A revitalized left politics would then grapple with constraints and openings rather than logics of power and history; it would develop strategies to counter specific regimes of rationality rather than countering specific policies within those regimes, on the one hand, or countering rationality as such, on the other.

Just as genealogy severs the links between "origins" and contemporary aims and purposes, so it also aims to sever critique from prescription.[34] This attempt to separate the question "what do we want to do" from the question "what kind of subjects are we, what political rationalities govern and shape us, and what political possibilities can we conjure from this condition" is not equivalent to the modernist conceit that critique can be cleansed of norms. We have already seen that genealogy is animated by political concerns and problematics. But the animating impulse may still be held apart from the question of what to do with the disruptions in our self-understanding that genealogy accomplishes. The political value of genealogy is its ability to call into question the most heavily naturalized features and encrusted relations of the present, to expose as a consequence of power what is ordinarily conceived as divinely, teleologically, or naturally ordained. Yet, what results from that exposé is a matter of political desire, political imagination, and political timing. Hence Foucault's general unwillingness to say what is to be done about punishment, sexual regulation, or the treatment of the mentally ill in his genealogies of these subjects. Put another way, Machiavelli becomes the exemplary theorist of political action and political alliance in the discursive political space opened by genealogy. For Machiavelli, history teaches us how to recognize political openings; but what kind of openings are sought and what is done with them is a matter of temperament, desire, imagination, skill, and luck.

. . . .

> [T]here is a very tenuous "analytic" link between a philosophical conception and the concrete political attitude of someone who is appealing to it; the "best" theories do not constitute a very effective protection against disastrous political choices.
> —Michel Foucault, "Politics and Ethics: An Interview"

In suggesting that Foucault's "politics" are the politics enabled by genealogy, I am quarreling with the notion that his own political affinities (variously labeled anarchist, libertarian, conservative, or neoliberal) and enthusiasms (May '68, prison reform, sexual deregulation, the Cambodian "boat people," the Iranian revolution) are the necessary outcome of genealogical studies or genealogical consciousness. A genealogical politics has no necessary political entailments: indeed, the particular kind of discursive space it affords for political thought, judgment, and political interventions is precisely a space free of the notion of necessary entailments. This characteristic is often considered a failing when viewed from a perspective in which legitimate political positions must flow directly from the endpoint of "objective" or "systematic" political critiques, but genealogy refuses this ruse and features instead forthrightly contingent elements of desire, attachment, judgment, and alliance as the compositional material of political attachments and positions.

Genealogy thus carves features of political space in an image parallel to its critique of conventional political and historical premises. Just as it is opposed methodologically to progressive accounts of history, unitary engines of history, and essentialized subjects of history, so when it opens the terrain for a postprogressivist politics, a postunitary politics, and a postidentity politics, it does not prescribe their replacements. Rather than opposing them on moral or political grounds (which would entail their alternatives), it generates a discursive political space for their interrogation. Insofar as genealogy contests a linear, progressive historical narrative, genealogical politics cannot deduce any necessary perspectives or future outcomes from any condition in the present. The present and its genealogy are instead grasped as the limiting conditions of political intervention and invention, not their governors. And much as genealogy contests a unified course of history with a map of "haphazard conflicts" and a "profusion of entangled events," so genealogical politics abandons the notion of a single party and a single direction for political opposition or political envisioning. Since genealogy problematizes essentialized feelings, sentiments, bodies, and subjects, since it treats all of these as historical effects, genealogical politics necessarily eschews any tight connection between the production of particular identities on the one hand and particular political positions or values on the other. An "ontology of the present" does not confuse itself with ontologically grounded politics.

Indeed, a critical ontology of the present could be precisely what productively disrupts or "cuts" the tight relation between constructions of identity and normative political claims in the contemporary political rationality.

The politics of Foucault's body of political, philosophical, and genealogical studies, I am arguing, cannot be linked to or inferred from Foucault's explicit political values, views, or attachments. The latter are a matter of contingent predilection; the political work his philosophical thinking can be made to do is relatively detachable from his preferences and could be attached to others. More generally, the politics of genealogy, as Nietzsche and Foucault craft them, are at best indeterminate. Genealogy aims to unfix the terms of the contemporary political situation, and it does so from a particular normative set of investments; but it doesn't tell us what is to be done, or even what is to be valued. It does not replace the truths and convictions it renders historically contingent and discursively containing; rather, it questions whether truths and convictions make up the right ethos for critical political consciousness.

Should these challenges constitute a source of political anxiety for left intellectuals? I think otherwise. Once the radical contingency of political views and judgments is avowed, it is possible to partially and productively depoliticize the theoretical enterprise without thereby rendering it apolitical. It becomes thinkable to distinguish between the political possibilities that a certain body of theory affords, the political uses to which it can be put, the political positions of the theorist, and a particular political deployment of the theory. *Political* truth then ceases to be sought *within* a particular theory but is, rather, that which makes an explicit bid for hegemony in the political realm. And theory may be allowed a return to its most fertile, creative, and useful place as, *inter alia*, an interlocutor of that domain.

SIX

■   ■   ■   ■

DEMOCRACY

Democracy against Itself:
Nietzsche's Challenge

Behold the good and the just! Whom do they hate most? The
man who breaks their table of values, the breaker, the law-
breaker; yet he is the creator.
> —Nietzsche, *Thus Spoke Zarathustra*

Whether we immoralists are harming virtue? Just as little as
anarchists harm princes. Only since the latter are shot at do
they again sit securely on their thrones. Moral: *morality must
be shot at.*
> —Nietzsche, *Twilight of the Idols*

We late moderns remain bound to a modernist habit of mea-
suring the political worth of thinkers by their proximity to the political
beliefs we are attached to; the tendency arises from an infelicitous
collapse of the political and the intellectual domains, a collapse itself
resulting from the radically insecure standing of each in modernity.[1]
Conventionally, the "politics" of a given theorist is identified either
with his or her explicit political views and alliances, that is, with political biography, or with the political values articulated in the theory
(democracy, socialism, individual liberty, community, and so forth),
that is, with political ideology.[2] And the politics of theory itself is generally judged by measures of relevance, applicability, or accessibility,
or it is debated in terms of features that are considered valuable—
abstraction, scientificity, universalism, and theorizing as such. In brief,
theory's value for politics is conventionally indexed by its capacity to
affect or predict political life, a capacity about which it is mostly defensive and against which it almost always comes up short.

To forge a different way of thinking about the theory-politics relation, and about the political value of particular theories and theorists, I propose that we affirm rather than deny the persistently untheoretical quality of politics—the resistance of political life to theory; the intercourse between politics and theory might then become more productive than one based on identity or application. If theory and politics consist of quite different, even conflicting, semiotic impulses and aims, perhaps we can conceive a usefully agonistic dynamic between them in order to avoid the more conventional relations of mutual condemnation, inadequacy, annoyance, or reproach. Let us take this risky hypothesis further: What if democratic politics, the most untheoretical of all political forms, paradoxically requires theory, requires an antithesis to itself in both the form and substance of theory, if it is to satisfy its ambition to produce a free and egalitarian order? What if democracy requires for its health a nondemocratic element, both because democracy is not an end in itself and because such an element is necessary if democracy is to avoid the most damnable things for which Plato, Nietzsche, and its other philosophical critics blame it? What if the anti-theoretical tendencies of democracy actually express a peculiar constitutive relation within democratic practice, an ambivalent relation of antagonism and dependence between democracy and theory that must be thematized and addressed directly if it is not to be corrosive of democracy?

In some always partial fashion, theory makes an object of everyday life and practices—and in that very gesture divests those practices of their everydayness, their lived and practical quality. In this simple sense, it is in the nature of the relation of politics and theory to distinguish themselves from each other: theory abstracts from political life and holds it up to examination, and thus cannot at the same time be identical with or even mirrored by it. But politics is also "untheoretical" and theory "unpolitical" in another sense. Among human practices, politics is peculiarly untheoretical because the bids for power that constitute it are necessarily at odds with the theoretical project of opening up meaning, of "making meaning slide," in Stuart Hall's words.[3] Discursive power functions by concealing the terms of its fabrication and hence its malleability and contingency; discourse fixes meaning by naturalizing it, or else ceases to have sway as discourse.[4]

This fixing or naturalizing of meanings is the necessary idiom in which politics takes place. Even the politics of deconstructive displacement implicates such normativity, at least provisionally. Pure deconstructive critique, while of inestimable value as a theoretical practice, is politically limited until and unless implications of the critique are developed in the political positing of new meanings (themselves subject to theoretical deconstruction).

Theory, in contrast, cannot fix meaning in this political fashion without ceasing to be theoretical, without sacrificing the dynamic action of theory, without falling into empiricism, positivism, or doctrine. For theory to live (the theorist "journeys in order to see," its Greek etymology reminds us), it must keep moving, it must keep taking critical distance from, and hence undoing, the terms of its objects. When theory aspires to fix meaning, then at the moment it believes itself to have defined definitively or chronicled exhaustively, it has made an object *in* the world, invested itself in that object and at that moment ceases to be theoretical. As politics does, theory undoes—but they are not necessarily opposites. A far more interesting relation is possible.

As Alexis de Tocqueville discerned, the relation of theory and politics in democracy is especially vexed. On the one hand, democracy is more antagonistic to theory than are most other regimes because of democracy's attachment to "common sense" and to its nervousness about elite knowledges. On the other hand, democracy needs theory more than other regimes, because of the democratic citizen's readiness to "trust the mass," with the result that "public opinion becomes more and more mistress of the world."[5] Still another paradox of democracy further complicates its relationship with theory, as a turn from Tocqueville to Spinoza reveals. According to Etienne Balibar, it is Spinoza who portrays democracy as unable "to find its own principle" despite functioning as an essential stabilizing element in other regimes. Spinoza can only define democracy itself as "a perfect aristocracy . . . an intrinsically contradictory concept."[6] This paradox results from the tension Spinoza posits, at the core of all regimes, between the state and mass (*imperium* and *multitudo*). Since pure democracy lacks this tension, insofar as state and mass are one, it negates itself as a regime.

Spinoza's argument about democracy's stabilizing function in non-democracies issues from his conviction that the tension between state and mass must be relaxed by some accord achieved between them, precisely the accord that a democratic element offers. Thus, the value of democracy is its equilibrating force in nondemocratic regimes, which cannot themselves manage the economy of energy and fear circulating between state and mass.[7] Balibar does not say that Spinoza denies the viability of democracy, only that he cannot locate a singular principle that defines, animates, and binds it *as* a regime; democracy thus becomes literally impossible for Spinoza to theorize. In Balibar's account of the unfinished character of the *Tractatus Politicus*, "we see [Spinoza] finally bogged down in a search for the 'natural' criteria of citizenship . . . and, if I dare say it, we watch him die before this blank page."[8]

Leaving aside the specifics of Spinoza's argument about the state-mass relationship, as well as the question of the relationship between Spinoza's terminal illness and his unfinished treatise on politics, let us consider the thesis that Spinoza's inability to theorize democracy is rooted in its lack of a principle of its own, and its consequent lack of material *for* theory. What if democracy is in fact missing what other regimes possess in principles such as excellence, *raison d'état*, imperial right, or property? Must democracy then be supplied a principle or purpose from outside? Must it be attached to a principle or principles other than itself, lest it become an amorphous and aimless rather than politically purposive entity—and become as well severely vulnerable to insurgency from within and conquest from without?

Again, Tocqueville's challenge would seem to parallel Spinoza's. Following his discussion of America's valorization of "individual understanding," Tocqueville describes the limit of this inclination for a body politic: "without ideas in common, no common action would be possible, and without common action, men might exist, but there could be no body social."[9] Yet since democracies *do* harbor social bodies, since they are not generally aimless, vulnerable, or even especially unstable, perhaps there is a vacuum in democracy that will inevitably be filled with a historically available principle—nationalism, racism, xenophobia, cultural chauvinism, market values, Christianity, imperialism, individualism, rights as ends—if some other principle is not more deliberately developed and pursued. While the principles to which modern democracy inadvertently attaches are not inherently dangerous and unsavory, they are likely to be so in fact if they are not formulated reflectively and deliberately, given the tendency in democracies both toward popular self-aggrandizement and toward the instrumentalist sensibility figured by rights and the market. Their imbrication with capitalism makes late modern liberal democracies especially prone to narcissistic decadence, bureaucratic domination, and technocracy, which in very different ways introduce markedly undemocratic forces into their midst. Though incapable of giving a specific name to the (capitalist) forces that would produce it, this was the condition Tocqueville forecast as the gloomy future of democracy at the close of his study of America:

> . . . I see an innumerable multitude of men, alike and equal, constantly circling around in pursuit of the petty and banal pleasures with which they glut their souls. Each one of them, withdrawn into himself, is almost unaware of the fate of the rest. Mankind, for him, consists in his children and his personal friends. . . . He exists in and for himself. . . . Over this kind of men stands an immense, protective power which is alone responsible for securing their enjoyment and watching over their fate. That power is absolute, provident, and gentle. . . . It gladly works for their happiness but wants to be sole agent and judge of it. . . . It covers the whole of social life with a network of petty, complicated rules that are both minute and uniform. . . . It does not break men's will, but softens, bends, and guides it . . . it is not at all tyrannical, but it hinders, restrains, enervates, stifles, and stultifies so much that in the end each nation is no more than a flock of timid and hardworking animals with the government as its shepherd.[10]

Theoretical self-consciousness may be deployed to interrupt democracy's relatively automatic cathexis onto undemocratic principles—it may provide at once enlightenment about this cathexis and a source of alternative principles. Thus, theory of a historically self-conscious sort may be a vehicle through which democracy can overcome itself without sacrificing itself, without turning against itself. Yet it would be a mistake to think that this use of theory can resolve the basic paradox of democracy formulated by Spinoza and Tocqueville. If democracy inherently lacks a principle of its own, then *any* principle brought to it will necessarily be antidemocratic: if democracy and principle are antithetical, if democracy is innately without a principle of its own, then any principle democracy attaches to must be partially at odds with it. It thus appears that the antidote for democracy's degenerative tendencies is homeopathic—it requires installing another antidemocratic element in democracy's heart. This is the paradox that brings theory and politics into specific relation in democracy, and the one for which Nietzsche's critique of democracy, as well as his more general critique of the political, may be rendered most useful.

The task of conceiving Nietzsche's value for democratic politics in this chapter, then, will wind around two related themes: the value of antidemocratic critique for democracy, and the value of theory for politics in terms other than those of application, method, ideology, or critique. Through Nietzsche, a consummately anti-political and undemocratic thinker, we may speculate about the value of theory for politics as a source of diagnosis, unlivable critique, and unreachable ideals rather than as a source of models, positions, or explanations of causes or origins. Again, in so doing, we must attend to a significant distinction between the character of politics and of theory. Recognizing such a distinction does not imply that there are no theoretical moments in politics and no politics to theory. Rather, it enables us to speculate that the prospect for a relationship useful to both may depend crucially on keeping their respective and admittedly mutable identities relatively aloof and autonomous even as they engage each other.

· · · ·

Conventional ways of locating Nietzsche's politics include examining the convergence of his thought with Nazi doctrine; his reduction of all demands for justice to envy; his misogyny, anti-Semitism, and racism; his heroic ethic and his esteem for ancient Athenian culture; his opprobrium toward the masses, democracy, socialism, and especially the sacred cow of modernity, political equality. Nietzsche has been variously characterized as anti-political, apolitical, and engaged in a "politics of transfiguration." He has been cast as deadly to politics, as a "haunt" or "conscience" to political thought and political life; as providing the ethos for a liberal ironism, for a recovery of moral-political responsibility, and for an agonistic liberal radicalism; and as a "way out" of Marxism, phenomenology, and existentialism in the twentieth century.[11] Most politically sympathetic treatments of Nietzsche try to draw a politics *out* of his thought, even as they recognize that there is much in Nietzsche that cannot be redeemed for democratic practice. But what if Nietzsche's thought is instead conceived as a knife to what covers the ideals and practices constitutive of political life? What if Nietzsche's thought does not guide but only provokes, reveals, and challenges, functioning in this way to strengthen democratic culture? Perhaps Nietzschean critiques and genealogies can *cut into* politics, productively interrupting, violating, or disturbing political formations rather than being applied to, merged with, or identified with them. This work would seem to be especially important for democratic politics, given my suggestion that democracy inevitably attaches to undemocratic elements and is also inhospitable to theory, including the theoretical self-consciousness required to grasp and redress the Spinozist point about democracy's hollow center.

To pursue these possibilities, we might first recall from the previous chapter Nietzsche the genealogical psychologist, the thinker who deploys speculative genealogies to probe the historical-psychological constitution of values such as justice, equality, or Christian morality. What is the significance of Nietzsche's diagnostic pose and genealogical approach for reconceiving the relationship of theory to politics? This question converges with those posed in the previous chapter: How does genealogy itself refigure the relation between the intellectual and the political? How does genealogy's crossing of philosophy and history open up the political present without itself taking the place of politics?

"We are unknown to ourselves, we men of knowledge," Nietzsche begins *On the Genealogy of Morals*, "and with good reason. We have never sought ourselves."[12] It is this ignorance that Nietzsche seeks to redress with his genealogical tracings of the desires (not only the unmediated will to power but its thwarted forms—envy, resentment, jealousy, and revenge) that materialize into the moral and political formations of equality, liberal justice, and the state. Unlike other genres of philosophical or historical criticism, including those delineated in his own *On the Advantage and Disadvantage of History for Life*, genealogy permits an examination of our condition that interrogates its very terms and construction. By doing violence to their ordinary ordering and situation, genealogy reveals the terms by which we live. In this way, the previous chapter argued, genealogy paradoxically aims to dislocate that which is both its starting point and its object: the present. And in the process, it also dislocates the conventions of politics, morality, and epistemology that constitute the present. The measure of genealogy's success is its disruption of conventional accounts of our identities, values, origins, and futures. Thus the project of deconstructing the inevitability, the naturalness, and the intractability of a time or a thing converges with the project of deconstructing the present as a culmination of the progress of the past, as well as with the exposure of power's operation in maintaining this particular present. None of these activities is equivalent to politics; it could even be argued that they are anti-political endeavors insofar as each destabilizes meaning without proposing alternative codes or institutions. Yet each may also be essential in sustaining an existing democratic regime by rejuvenating it. For the vertigo that genealogy aims to achieve may amount to the very measure of how far collective or individual identity can be dissolved in order to disrupt without destroying, to offer the possibility of resolving into another story.

Why would anyone actively seek to dissolve or destabilize identity within democracies? If, as the musings of Spinoza and Tocqueville suggest, democracies tend toward cathexis onto principles antithetical to democracy, then critical scrutiny of these principles and of the political formations animated by them is crucial to the project of refounding or recovering democracy. What Machiavelli casts as the "return of a republic to its beginnings"[13] might here be supplemented with the notion of a theoretical endeavor, genealogy, that continuously examines and reworks both the founding principles and powers of a polity and those principles and powers with which it has since become interwoven. Identity dissolution, achieved theoretically, is thus a means of asking whether we are who or what we want to be, a means of evaluating the principles by which we order ourselves—in short, a means of interrupting that tendency in democracy to adhere without reflection to nondemocratic principles or practices, and to be inhabited by nondemocratic powers. Significantly, the challenge to identity that genealogy offers is not equivalent to political dissolution—it questions without destroying or prohibiting a particular formation of collective identity. Again, genealogy is not politics but a register of reflection on it; its effect is to disturb political space and political formations rather than to claim such space or create such formations on its own. In refiguring the relations among history, philosophy, and politics, genealogy shapes the meeting of theory and politics as mutual experience of incitation or provocation.

While Nietzsche's genealogical inquiry can be drawn with relative ease into the project of political self-scrutiny and debate, a more familiar Nietzsche establishes philosophy and politics as flatly rejecting one another and describes both in wholly unflattering terms. In *Twilight of the Idols*, Nietzsche polemicizes against philosophers and philosophy as antilife. The philosophical inquiries of Socrates and Plato are condemned as "symptoms of degeneration or decay" in Greek life, since to "judge the value of life" itself constitutes a negation of life.[14] Dialectics is characterized as poor manners—"the revenge of the rabble"—and specious thought: "honest things . . . do not carry their reasons exposed in this fashion" (p. 31). More generally, Socratic philosophy is portrayed as an expression of *ressentiment* that devitalizes its opponents. "As long as life is *ascending*, happiness equals instinct"; whereas philosophy reproaches the senses, the body, the instincts, and history as deceivers about the "true world"—they draw us into the world of becoming, the world of appearance (pp. 33, 34). This reproach of life voiced by Greek philosophy, Nietzsche argues, was a pathological response to the "anarchy of the instincts" accompanying Athens' decline:

If one needs to make a tyrant of *reason*, as Socrates did, then there must exist no little danger of something else playing the tyrant. . . . The fanaticism with which the whole of Greek thought throws itself at rationality betrays a state of emergency. . . . The moralism of the

Greek philosophers from Plato downwards is pathologically conditioned. . . . Reason = virtue = happiness means merely: one must imi-
tate Socrates and counter the dark desires by producing a permanent
daylight—the daylight of reason. (pp. 32–33)

For Nietzsche, the decadence of the Greek philosophers, expressed as
hyperrationality, is a *symptom* of the decline of Greece's greatness:
"the philosophers are the decadents of Hellenism, the counter-move-
ment against the old, the noble taste (against the agonal instinct,
against the *polis*, against the value of the race, against the authority
of tradition)" (p. 108). In the decline of Athens, Nietzsche discerns
the more general tendency of philosophy toward revenge and *ressentiment*, its assault on that before which it feels small and humiliated.
Out of its experience of impotence or injury vis-à-vis public life or
culture, philosophy seeks to substitute itself for them, to displace and
replace rather than engage them. Here, Plato is his exemplar.

Though Nietzsche frequently generalizes from this depiction of philosophy in Greek culture in order to insist that philosophy as such is
antilife, Nietzschean philosophy, often masquerading as allegory or
psychological maxims, also aims to provoke the spirit of overcoming
that affirms humanity. Nietzsche's polemic against philosophy is thus
at the same time a call for a philosophy of a different sort. His critique
of philosophy centers on the unself-conscious will to power in it that
potentially vanquishes its object—man—in an effort to dominate that
object. But this same will to power makes philosophy a potent instrument of other values as well; indeed, it animates Nietzsche's own philosophical moves against the philosophers he criticizes.

If, in the name of "life," Nietzsche bears some ambivalence toward
philosophy, there is no such ambiguity in his open hostility toward
politics, which includes moral doctrines such as equality, institutions
such as the state and political parties, career politicians, righteous
position-taking, and policy making. Nietzsche's objections to moral
political doctrine, especially that of liberalism, include his notorious
disdain for the rabble and for the "little men" whose envious, petty,
and poisonous nature, he believes, sap all strength from a culture.[15]
Nietzsche's critique of political solutions to "unfairness" and other
moralizing claims against domination is distilled in his forthright

claim: " 'Men are not equal.' . . . Life wants to climb and to overcome itself climbing."[16] If liberal doctrine thus inevitably partakes of
slave morality, when this critique is compounded by Nietzsche's loath-
ing of the state—the "coldest of all cold monsters[,] . . . where the
slow suicide of all is called 'life' "[17]—then all modern state-centered
political formations, whether socialist, democratic, or totalitarian, appear even more antagonistic than is philosophy to "life" and culture.
"The better the state is established," Nietzsche polemicizes, "the
fainter is humanity."[18]

Even these critiques do not plumb the depths of Nietzsche's hostility
to politics, a hostility many have termed aesthetic or cultural but that
might be better understood as an intense anti-institutionalism rooted
in his critique of slave morality. " 'The will to power' is so loathed in
democratic ages," he argues, "that the whole of the psychology of
these ages seems directed towards its belittlement and slander."[19] In
Twilight of the Idols, Nietzsche emphasizes the massified, de-individu-
alizing character of democratic institutions, the way in which they
lose "man" in a regime putatively designed to protect "everyman":
" 'Equality' . . . belongs essentially to decline: the chasm between man
and man, class and class, the multiplicity of types, the will to be oneself, to stand out—that which I call *pathos of distance*—characterizes
every *strong* age. The tension, the range between the extremes is today
growing less and less—the extremes themselves are finally obliterated
to the point of similarity" (p. 91). This appreciation of distance—not
simply hierarchy—as culturally invigorating emerges in Nietzsche's
characterization of freedom as "the will to self-responsibility" that
"preserves the distance which divides us" (p. 92).

Like Foucault, Nietzsche charges modern politics with excessively
organizing and institutionalizing human relations. This institutional-
ism dissolves our distinctiveness, our separateness, even as it fabricates
us as "individuals"; it throws us into proximity in a fashion that mutes
our own capacity to be active, creative, and hence free; it sacrifices the
energy of free creatures, indeed of expressivism, to a homogenizing
proceduralism. Like Rousseau, Nietzsche regards mass social intercourse and the institutions that perpetuate it as enemies of discerning
sensibilities and values. Thus tolerance, one of democracy's proudest
virtues, emerges as a symptom of its baseness. "To put up with men,

to keep open house in one's heart—this is liberal, but no more than liberal. One knows hearts which are capable of *noble* hospitality, which have curtained windows and closed shutters: they keep their best rooms empty . . . because they await guests with whom one does *not* have to put up" (p. 82). For Nietzsche, to regard all indifferently, to treat everyone as if they were equally deserving of respect, is a sign less of magnanimity or of an egalitarian sensibility than of the incapacity to judge what and who are of value.

In short, Nietzsche regards political life, especially modern political life, as harboring values and spawning institutions that displace and discourage individual *and* collective aspiration, creativity, distinction, and cultural achievement. The state is "*unmorality* organized," a "huge machinery" that "quells the individual," substituting instead a mechanical individualism in which all are reduced to units.[20] Political parties are for unthinking followers—"he who thinks much is not suited to be a party member: too soon, he thinks himself through and beyond the party."[21] And modern political doctrines are mostly justifications of and for the weak against the strong, or for the rational against the Dionysian, issuing in either case from *ressentiment*.[22]

Nietzsche's critique of politics should also be read in relation to his chosen signifier of human redemption, culture. While Nietzsche concedes a potentially synergistic relation between politics and culture when the former itself partakes of "greatness" (Periclean Athens is the ambivalent example that he frequently cites), politics is more often cast as a straightforward enemy of culture. Insisting that modern justice claims are born of envy or other elements of slave morality, and that nationalism and anarchy draw on the least admirable mobilization of desire, Nietzsche celebrates war as the only element of political life that is potentially ennobling for the collective spirit.[23] He sees the antagonism of politics to culture as arising not only from the former's cultivation of herd morality but also from its tendency to fix or stabilize its domain via enervating institutions: "Like every organizational political power, the Greek *polis* spurned and distrusted the increase of culture among its citizens; its powerful natural impulse was to do almost nothing but cripple and obstruct it. The *polis* did not want to permit to culture any history or evolution; the education determined by the law of the land was intended to bind all generations and keep them at one level. . . . So culture developed *in spite* of the *polis*."[24]

Nietzsche's negative view of institutions generally—like that of his twentieth-century student, Foucault—is linked to his belief that institutions contain and constrain life, dominating through excessive control and devitalization of their subjects. With similarities to Max Weber's account of routinized charisma and Sheldon Wolin's critique of constitutionalized democracy,[25] Nietzsche offers a formulation in which the very aim of institutions to endure, secure, and routinize renders them at odds with a cultural ethos of creativity, struggle, and overcoming. Thus, Nietzsche jokes, "the overthrow of beliefs is not immediately followed by the overthrow of institutions; rather the new beliefs live for a long time in the now desolate and eerie house of their predecessors, which they themselves preserve, because of the housing shortage."[26] For Nietzsche, modern political institutions inevitably aim to fix and stabilize; they achieve a kind of static domination—indeed, a domination that is achieved through the containment of change—as well as invest the world with the *ressentiment* of justice shaped by envy and a reproach of power. Culture, by contrast, represents the prospect of innovation, aspiration, and creative effort. Like theory, culture climbs, slides, and functions to undo meaning, conventional practices, and, above all, institutions. Culture harbors not merely the prospect of greatness but a spirit of freedom, which, according to Nietzsche, political life can never offer.

. . . .

Now, what if instead of defending politics and democracy against Nietzsche's critiques, which most democrats, radical or liberal, are understandably wont to do, we allowed these critiques the force of a partial and provisional truth—a discomforting, undemocratic truth—and attempted to discern how they might enrich democratic political projects? "Whatever doesn't kill me makes me stronger," Nietzsche taunts,[27] perhaps providing a clue about how criticism might invigorate rather than demolish its object.

Another way of putting the problem: What use for thinking about the relation of theory and politics is a philosopher who is hostile to both in the name of something called "life" or culture? Nietzsche's insistence on the limiting force of both theory and politics does not prevent their productive intercourse to produce an illness—"as pregnancy is an illness," in one of his provocative maxims.[28] Although it is peripheral to his own purposes, in Nietzsche we can find the basis for an agonistic interlocution between theory and politics, especially in democracies, which I have suggested are inherently anti-theoretical and lacking in any binding principle. Politics and theory can question each other without having to answer to each other—without becoming either identical or even mutually accountable.[29] I am further suggesting that politics, which relentlessly fixes meanings and generates their consolidation in institutions, requires theory's anti-political rupture of these meanings and institutions in order not to become the nightmare of human sociality, power brokering, and discursive banality that politics always threatens to become. The realm of politics needs to be cut through by counterforces both to incite its virtues and, in a technocratic age, to derail its slide into a historically unprecedented machinery of domination.

A productive relation between theory and politics might be conceived on the model of Nietzschean friendship. "In a friend one should still honor the enemy. Can you go close to your friend without going over to him? You should be closest to him with your heart when you resist him."[30] Can theory and politics manage such *amour*? It would require affirming the relative autonomy, value, and strength of each, *believing* in them, and restoring good faith in them. Such a relation also calls forth from democracy what does not come easily to it: namely, *effort*, the struggle to overcome itself that is also the means by which it can save itself from turning into its opposite. Democracy's lack of a principle means that it risks having nothing that is "difficult"; and what is most difficult for the spirit, Nietzsche insists in *Zarathustra*, is what the spirit's *strength* demands.[31] This means not that democracy must have a difficult principle at its heart in order to have a strong spirit, but that the struggle between democratic and antidemocratic impulses—between political constraints and imperatives and antidemocratic theoretical disruptions, between egalitarian and inegalitarian desires, between affirmations of strength and limitations of it—can be invigorating rather than dangerous for democracy if righteous platitudes and attitudes are not deployed to quell that struggle.

In the form in which he offers it, Nietzsche's critique of democracy is largely unlivable. No matter what its modality—socialist, liberal, or communitarian—modern democratic life in state societies cannot be conducted with shuttered rooms and aristocratic practices that disregard most of humanity; it cannot be allied with contempt for the many nor with reduction of all egalitarian doctrine to envy and resentment. So rather than embracing this critique, could we employ it as a provocation, an incitement? Could democratic institutions and practices be productively challenged with what Nietzsche called a noble sensibility, one that discriminates and discerns, that aspires to greatness and shuns petty ambition and petty injury? Indeed, how might democracy not merely harbor such apparently antidemocratic values as a practice of tolerance but cultivate them as a means of preventing itself from sliding into technocracy on one side, and base attachments or principles on the other? To ask this question in a different register: What might be the *force* of theory as "anti-politics" in renewing democratic political life that has decayed from within, withered by its own excessive institutionalization and perhaps more occupied by the spirit of "slave morality" than we like to admit?

There is an entirely different way in which Nietzsche's critique could be a source of democratic renewal. Genealogy is uniquely suited to bring to light a specific democracy's historical attachments to and imbrications with nondemocratic principles. Genealogy challenges conceits of purity: through it, particular democracies are revealed as enfolded within histories of imperialism, slavery, genocide, class dominance, or punishment and as saturated with these legacies in the present. In this regard, genealogy calls to account the institutions of democracies, indeed challenging the institutionalization of democracy itself insofar as it always entails both an attenuation of popular power *and* an incorporation of antidemocratic populist values. It is this institutionalization that Nietzsche condemned as antilife and especially antifreedom, and that others have critically interrogated as incompatible with democracy understood as the perpetual sovereignty of the people, as the continuous practice of freedom.[32]

Nietzsche's theoretical challenges to democracy become important in still another way, serving as challenges to democratic values themselves. Particularly in late modernity, when liberal democracy in the particular form given by contemporary capitalism is all that remains standing in a history of tried-and-failed regimes, liberal democracy risks more than ever a laconic, self-satisfied tendency, avoiding "what is difficult" both because its anti-theoretical nature produces no internal calls for an accounting and because it faces no ideological challenges from without. Democracy lives its many paradoxes without featuring the struggle over them as its potential life force, its potential greatness. Liberal democracy rarely submits its cardinal values of mass equality and tolerance to interrogation without dismissing such challenges as antidemocratic; nor does it seriously engage critiques of its tendency to subordinate all elements of life to market domination and political egalitarianism. Consequently, even as we may admire our widely accessible contemporary technologies and cultural productions, we cast sidelong glances across a seemingly unbridgeable chasm at the grand cultural masterpieces produced by the elites of previous centuries, without asking whether what Nietzsche designated as culture's antipathy to the democratic sentiment could be made a useful interlocutor of democracy, offering precisely the challenge that might lead democracy to "climb" in the manner Nietzsche insisted was the sole purview of culture. Matters are complex here: while the contemporary force of political egalitarianism produces a certain kind of social leveling and rule by administration, the force of the market (to which Nietzsche was hardly attentive) produces radical social inequality as well as a form of "culture" that is far from the sort Nietzsche associated with greatness and striving. So the Nietzschean challenge on the subject of culture would have to undergo a transformation before it could be made useful to contemporary democracy: what is harbored within the Nietzschean notion of culture that could be deployed to challenge both liberal democratic and market values, thereby inciting a richer practice both of democracy *and* of culture than that which is currently engendered by liberalism and capitalism?

In the spirit of such a reformulation of Nietzsche's thought as a haunt to democracy, let us return to a theme raised at the beginning of this chapter by Tocqueville and by Balibar's reading of Spinoza. If democracy is governance by the people, and the people as a political mass are figured as the opposite of the state, no modern democracy can persist without the state form; perhaps it is this paradox that Nietzschean philosophy helps us stage as political possibility rather than entrapment. Permanent resistance to the state that simultaneously constitutes democracy and is one of the chief sources of democracy's dissolution becomes a means of sustaining democracy.[33] Only through the state are the people constituted as a people; only in resistance to the state do the people remain a people. Thus, just as democracy requires antidemocratic critique in order to remain democratic, so too the democratic state may require democratic resistance rather than fealty if it is not to become the death of democracy. Similarly, democracy may require theory's provision of unlivable critiques and unreachable ideals. In order not to become profoundly undemocratic, democracy requires external incitement to efforts, principles, and aims that it can neither provide for itself nor fulfill without losing itself. If this array of difficult paradoxes composes Nietzsche's mixed bouquet to democratic aspirations, then perhaps Nietzsche is the antidemocratic thinker whom democracy cannot live without.

SEVEN

■　■　■　■

FUTURES

Specters and Angels: Benjamin and Derrida

A Klee painting named "Angelus Novus" shows an angel
looking as though he is about to move away from something
he is fixedly contemplating. His eyes are staring, his mouth is
open, his wings are spread. This is how one pictures the angel
of history. His face is turned toward the past. Where we perceive a chain of events, he sees one single catastrophe which
keeps piling wreckage upon wreckage and hurls it in front of
his feet. The angel would like to stay, awaken the dead, and
make whole what has been smashed. But a storm is blowing
from Paradise; it has got caught in his wings with such violence that the angel can no longer close them. This storm irre-
sistibly propels him into the future to which his back is
turned, while the pile of debris before him grows skyward.
This storm is what we call progress.
 —Walter Benjamin, "Theses on the Philosophy of History"

If Benjamin's generation was forced to recognize that "capitalism will not die a natural death," ours has had to learn the
further lesson that capitalism is not, for the foreseeable future, going to die at all.
 —Irving Wohlfarth, "The Measure of the Possible, the
  Weight of the Real, and the Heat of the Moment"

From every area of contemporary discourse, we know that the
pace of contemporary social, cultural, economic, and political change
is unprecedented. Technological obsolescence occurs at the inception
of production, deracination in human lives is ubiquitous and normal,
divorce rates have almost caught up with marriage rates, yesterday's
deal is history, today's corporate giant is the material of tomorrow's
dissolved or merged identity. If all that was solid melted into air in the
last century, today's economic, social, and technological transforma-

tions occur so rapidly that they often do not even achieve solidity before metamorphosing into something else. This much we know and recount to ourselves regularly. But we do not know much about the relationship of this pace of change to the history that shapes and constrains it, nor to the future that it heralds. On a daily basis we live the paradox that the most rapid-paced epoch in human history harbors a future that is both radically uncertain and profoundly beyond the grasp of the inhabitants of the present. Moving at such speed without any sense of control or predictability, we greet both past and future with bewilderment and anxiety. As a consequence, we inheritors of a radically disenchanted universe feel a greater political impotence than humans may have ever felt before, even as we occupy a global order more saturated by human power than ever before. Power without purpose, power without lines of determination, power without end in every sense of the word.

Perhaps at no other historical moment has Benjamin's angel been such a poignant signifier of our predicament. Without vision or a strong sense of agency, we are blown backward into the future as debris piles up in the single catastrophe that is history beyond and outside of human invention or intervention, a history of both dramatic and subtle unfreedom. We cannot close our wings against the storm, cannot not be moved—that moment has been extinguished by contemporary history itself. Our capacity to intervene in the trajectory and the wide range of effects of capital (as the most powerful moving force in modernity), to whatever extent it once existed, appears exhausted. So history surges on, but with no promise that past suffering will be redeemed, with no promise of eventual worldwide or even local emancipation, well-being, wisdom, or reduction of suffering. *Nihilistic* seems far too thin a term to describe such circumstances.

How are we to rectify this condition, which is to say, how are we to rectify our impotence in the face of a present and future of driven, rushing aimlessness? Part of the answer lies in how we might refigure the relation of the present to the past, how we might articulate the mass and force of the past in the present when they can no longer be captured by a progressive narrative. At stake in this rethinking are two questions: what kind of historical consciousness is possible and appropriate for contemporary political critique and analysis, and how can agency be derived to make a more just, emancipatory, or felicitous future order. To see how urgently answers to both are needed, we might consider two instances of contemporary anxiety and confusion about historical political thinking, one drawn from the political domain and one from academic debates.

In contemporary political parlance, the relation of the present to the past is most often figured through idealizations and demonizations of particular epochs or individuals on the one hand, and reparations and apologies for past wrongs on the other. Especially with regard to the latter, we might ask what this figuring covers over, defers, or symptomatizes in the present. How does it elide the most difficult questions about the bearing of the past on the present? German repayments to European Jewish estates looted in the 1930s, White House apologies to African Americans for enslaving or mistreating them, state compensation to Japanese Americans from California sent to internment camps during World War II, lawsuits concerning reparations to Native Americans for stolen lands and breached treaties, China's resentment about Japan's failure to issue a written apology for its atrocities in the 1930s, even civil litigation by families who have suffered from wrongful verdicts in murder trials—what is the significance of conceiving historical trauma in terms of guilt, victimization, and, above all, reparation and apology? Once guilt is established and a measure of victimization secured by an apology or by material compensation, is the historical event presumed to be concluded, sealed as past, "healed," or brought to "closure"? Is this referral to the law and to an economy of debt and payment a way of attempting to designate the past as really past, and to liberate the present from that past? What anxiety about the way these past traumas *live* in the present might be signified by such impulses to resolve them through a discursive structure of wrong, debt, and payment?

Another sign of contemporary anxiety about history's bearing on the present appears in a particular mode of criticizing poststructuralist challenges to the status of materiality and objectivity in history. Responding to formulations that challenge notions of brute facticity and that, more generally, call into question objectivist or positivist accounts of history, many of these critics proclaim: "But the Holocaust really happened! It involved massive dislocation, human slaughter,

and obliteration of communities, estates, artifacts, and archives."
There are two important political questions begged in the rejoinder
that something "happened" in history: First, what account of this happening has the most veracity and why? Second, what are the meanings
of this historical occurrence for political and cultural life in the present? It is the second of these questions that concerns us here. Of course
the Holocaust happened, but to itemize the devastation that it
wrought tells us nothing about what it means for those who, sixty
years later, live in its historical aftermath in different ways in different
parts of the world. Thus, an insistence on the materiality or facticity
of the Holocaust is just as dodgy about the question of how the Holocaust lives in the present as it claims its putative opposition to be. The
questions about history that matter for the political present are not
answered by a factually precise accounting of the North American
slave trade in the nineteenth century, or by a listing of the homosexu-
als, gypsies, Jews, and communists killed by European fascists in the
1930s and 1940s. Rather, the political questions produced by the current crisis in historiography and by the breakdown of a progressive
historical metanarrative include these: How do the histories of slavery,
colonialism, or Nazism in North America and Europe contour contemporary political, social, and cultural life? How do these histories
constrain, produce, or occupy the present? No empirical or materialist
history can answer these questions, yet that very failing appears to be
what such histories are warring against both in their claims to truth
and in their reproaches of those histories that call into question the
possibility of an empirically "true" account. The complex *political*
problem of the relation between past and present, and of both to the
future, is resolved by neither facts nor truth. While scholars of postcolonial orders understand this well, precisely because colonial histories
discursively suffuse the postcolonial present so overtly, it is no small
irony that the hegemonic historiography of the metropoles still holds
out objectivity as a form of historical and political salvation.

One problem framing this chapter thus concerns the failure of conventional historiographies to provide useful maps for developing historically conscious political orientation in the present; the second concerns the ground of political motivation in the present, perhaps most
succinctly characterized as a crisis in what Hannah Arendt termed

"love of the world."[1] Ours is a present that is hurtled into the future without regard for human attachments, needs, or capacities. A present that dishonors the past by erasing it with unprecedented speed and indifference. A present that equates the recent past with the anachronistic, with insufficient *technē* to survive. A present in which a knowledgeable politician is a policy wonk rather than a reader of political histories. A present whose inevitable and rapid eclipse is uppermost in the political consciousness of its inhabitants. How can such a present be loved—and if it cannot be, what are our investments in addressing its ills? What is there to attach to in a world of such incessant and rapid transformations? How can one sufficiently love the world generated by this present to want to do right by it? From what depth of feeling, conventionally cultivated through lifelong and generations-old attachments and values, can such a time be simultaneously embraced—providing the basis for love and loyalty—and challenged—providing the basis for political activism? If there are no such sources of continuity to draw on, then from what wellspring do we affirm our time, engage our dilemmas, define our imperatives? What incites our grievances and spurs our hopes?

A time of incessant change, Sheldon Wolin reminds us, is also a time saturated with loss. In his consideration of "invocation" as a figure for the potential value of political theory and political theorists, he recalls that invocation in ancient Rome "was an appeal to a departed deity," an effort to recover something lost. Thus, as a practice, "invocation may be said to imply memory and to enjoin recovery."[2] Walter Benjamin, writing half a century earlier in another era that both confounded the modernist ideal of progress and harbored unfathomable orders of power and loss, invoked an angel to refigure the presence of the past in political thought. The angel signified memory and reparation as well as despair, hope, and a disguised meaning in—and thus a partial redemption of—human suffering. More recently, Jacques Derrida has revisited Marx's texts to develop an image of the present as inhabited by specters and ghosts of the past and future. Deities, angels, specters, and ghosts . . . what are we to make of these creatures rising from the pens of radical thinkers in the twentieth century as they attempt to grasp our relation to the past and future, and in particular as they attempt to articulate the prospects for a postfoundational formulation of justice? What leads a radical democrat to speak of deities, a Marxist literary critic to invoke angels, and a deconstructive philosopher of language to speak of specters and argue for a practice of "hauntology"? What must be exhausted in certain strains of secular, progressive thought for quasi-theological figures conventionally opposed to such thought, and deposed by it, to be made to seem valuable, perhaps even essential?

This chapter explores these questions indirectly, by considering Derrida's and Benjamin's reflections on the problems of historical consciousness—the relation of the past to the present, to memory, to loss, and hence to the future. Derrida's *Specters of Marx* offers an imaginative reading of selected texts by Marx and, by way of that reading, a critique of conventional understandings of Marx's contemporary legacy. Through this reading, too, Derrida endeavors to reconceive the press of history on the present, an endeavor that may break even more radically with progressive historiography than does genealogy as formulated by Nietzsche and Foucault. In his porous schema of spectrality that includes ghosts, haunting, and conjuration, Derrida experiments with a mode of historical consciousness that does not resort to discredited narratives of systematicity, periodicity, laws of development, or a bounded, coherent past and present. Derrida is also attentive to the problem of political judgment and political hope, and he attempts to establish a terrain for both without locating either in a narrative of progress or founding either in metaphysical precepts.

In "Theses on the Philosophy of History" and other meditations on historical consciousness, Benjamin provides a critique of progress, reworks the meaning of historical materialism through that critique, and offers grounds—or at least handholds or windows on possibility—for revolutionary political action. But Benjamin is not only a critic of modernist political conventions such as progress and materialist metaphysics; he is also the consummate theorist (poet) of political despair who mines a unique strain of hopefulness from the very same terrain. He is thus a theorist who promises a transformative orientation toward our contemporary political paralysis and suffering, which are framed by the combination of speed, unprecedented amounts of unharnessed power, an aimlessness of historical direction, and the resulting experience of impotence described above. Benjamin's location of historical consciousness "within the cultural work of mourning" allows for the possibility of redeeming historical losses, a redemption that conventionally melancholic attachments to those losses would foreclose.[3] Achieving this redemption through what Benjamin terms an "activation" of the past opens new possibilities in the present as well. Together, Derrida's and Benjamin's writings on history offer partial strategies for configuring responsible political consciousness and political agency in the unsettling and unsettled time after progress.

DERRIDA'S *SPECTERS OF MARX*

How do we figure history at the end of (modern) history, when the presumption that history progresses has been exposed epistemologically as theological and is experienced practically as a cruel hoax? What is history's postprogressive shape, weight, and force, and what language can best express those parameters? What kind of historical discourse is not merely antiprogressive (as genealogy is sometimes said to be "Whig history in reverse") but disrupts a progressive narrative by relocating historical meaning into some other space and idiom? That is, what discourse of history provides a way of conceiving the relationship between past, present, and future without setting its compass points through or against a discourse of progress? For Derrida, these questions are threaded through a historically specific question about Marx: how do we figure both Marx's thinking and Marx's legacy outside of a progressive historiography, when the history of Marxism in a progressive vein has literally come to an end, when Marxism as political possibility and political imperative (and Derrida will tolerate no version of Marx's thought that is less politically invested) died a decade ago? Derrida's reading of Marx against conventional Marxist historiography is thus simultaneously a reading of Marx against Marxism and a reading of Marx against present-day anti-Marxists who celebrate Marxism's death. Derrida aims to deprive the present of its sense of triumph over Marxism, its sense of being done with Marxism—a sense he believes Marxism has colluded in through its own historiography, its own wager on progress.

We begin with a question Derrida poses lightly across his text: Are ghosts and spirits what inevitably arise at the end or death of something—an era, desire, attachment, belief, figure, or narrative? When we have arrived at the putative end of history, should it surprise us if history reappears in the form of a haunt? Put differently, when we cease to figure history in terms of laws, drives, development, or logic, are ghosts what remain? What, precisely, is the nature and content of this remainder? The grounding of Derrida's query is only in part psychoanalytic—the assumption that suppression, repression, and the logic of mourning govern consciousness. It issues as well from his speculative philosophical musings about death—how death affects the living, how the dead live among the living, how the past lives indirectly in the present, inchoately suffusing and shaping rather than determining it. For Derrida, the very language of haunting, the fact that we possess this language, is our confession that dead things live; ghosts contravene the finality of death for the living, undoing the line between death and life.

Derrida records his own beginning with this text: "Someone, you or me, comes forward and says: I would like to learn to live finally."[4] Learning to live, Derrida insists, involves first accepting that life and death are not opposed; this non-opposition is conventionally figured by ghosts, the live figures of the dead who suggest one form of life after death. Thus in learning to live, which entails embracing the non-opposition of death to life, "it would be necessary to learn spirits" (p. xvii): to learn when, how, and why they appear and how we conjure or invoke them. Affirming this non-opposition also entails living without conceits of foundations, origins, and progress, and especially without clear distinctions between the real and the fictive, the ideal and the material, the past and the present. Learning to live without all of these props in turn means learning to practice ethical conduct and pursue political justice within a world that is contingent, unpredictable, not fully knowable, and directed neither by external forces nor by internal logics. Again, the figure Derrida offers for this practice is learning to live with haunts or specters—with things that shape the present, rendering it as always permeated by an elsewhere but in a fashion that is inconstant, ephemeral, and hence not fully mappable.

Ghosts thus emblematize a postmetaphysical way of life, a way of life saturated by elements—could we call them "material conditions"?—that are not under our sway and that also cannot be harnessed to projects of reason, development, progress, or structure. Ghosts figure the impossibility of mastering, through either knowledge or action, the past or the present. They figure the necessity of grasping certain implications of the past for the present only as traces or effects (rather than as structures, axioms, laws, or lines of determination) and of grasping even these as protean. "Learning to live finally" means learning to live with this unmasterable, uncategorizable, and irreducible character of the past's bearing on the present, and hence with the unmasterable and irreducible character of the present as well. Learning to live means living without systematizing, without conceits of coherence, without a consistent and complete picture, and without a clear delineation between past and present. Living with ghosts, permitting and even exploiting their operation as a deconstructive device, means living with the permanent disruption of the usual oppositions that render our world coherent—between the material and the ideal, the past and the present, the real and the fictive, the true and the false. Ghosts are what rise from materialism, periodicity, and objectivity after each has been slain by the exposure of their untenable predicates. We quarrel with these ghosts and also with one another about them—their shape, their meaning, their significance, their longevity. Both kinds of quarrels affirm and produce the existence of ghosts; neither kind stabilizes the meaning of the past for the present.

In asking what it would mean to "learn to live finally," Derrida intends to ask not only about a viable postfoundational epistemological orientation and individual ethical pose, but also about political orientation and especially matters of justice.

> The time of the "learning to live," a time without tutelary present, would amount to this . . .: to learn to live with ghosts, in the upkeep, the conversation, the company, or the companionship, in the commerce without commerce of ghosts. To live otherwise and better. No, not better, but more justly. But with them. No *being-with* the other, no *socius* without this *with* that makes *being-with* in general more enigmatic than ever for us. And this being-with specters would also be, not only but also, a politics of memory, of inheritance and of generations.

No justice . . . seems possible or thinkable without the principle
of some responsibility, beyond all living present, within that which
disjoins the living present, before the ghosts of those who are not yet
born or who are already dead. . . . Without this non-contemporane-
ity with itself of the living present, without that which secretly un-
hinges it, without this responsibility and this respect for justice concerning those who are not there, of those who are no longer or who
are not yet present and living, what sense would there be to ask the
question "where?" "where tomorrow?" "whither?" (pp. xviii–xix)

Derrida's formulation of justice here breaks with the usual conventions in political theory. It has little relation to a distributional definition; nor is it procedural, rights oriented, tethered to law, or even tied
to measures of participation or shared power. Rather, justice in this
text is less institutional or spatial than temporal: it pertains almost
entirely to a practice of responsible relations between generations.[5]
Justice concerns not only our debt to the past but also the past's legacy
in the present; it informs not only our obligation to the future but also
our responsibility for our (ghostly) presence in that future. "Justice
carries life beyond present life or its actual being there" (p. xx). Justice
demands that we locate our political identity between what we have
inherited and what is not yet born, between what we can only imagine
and the histories that constrain and shape that imagination. This is a
notion of political identity quite at odds with an identity shaped by
fixed social coordinates and especially by group affinity. Justice, Derrida argues, is literally incoherent if dehistoricized, detached from futurity, or confined to a self-identical present. But not only must justice
have futurity—it is what *makes* futurity, insofar as it generates the
future's relationship to the present as a "living on" of present efforts
and aims. Justice entails the present generation's responsibility for
crafting continuity, as well as the limits of that responsibility and that
continuity.

How can one argue for the imperative of this continuity without
relying on the usual moral and historiographic ruses? Such an argument is Derrida's political project with the specter: namely, the figuring of a novel mode of temporality as a basis for political responsibility, a mode that honors and redeems the past without recourse to *Geist*

(or any other logic of history) and that is also responsive to imagined future generations, even offering them a certain promise and guarantee without pretending that it can orchestrate their relations. Derrida proffers this strange and intangible figure of the specter as a site of renewal for historical consciousness and political agency after all modernist logics of history and political change have given up the ghost.

Conceived spectrally, the present-past relation recasts not only the weight and force of the past in the present but vital elements of the political present as well. As we shall see, Derrida exploits the specter's quality of "in-betweenness" to disrupt certain modernist formulations of ontology, theology, epistemology, and teleology that undergird conventional forms of political critique and political value tethered to a stable notion of the present. The specter as the "becoming body" challenges ontology as fixity, and challenges as well the distinction between material dimension and concept. The specter as a "carnal form of spirit" disrupts both an otherworldly and an idealist formulation of theology and the subject; at the same time, it undoes the materiality conventionally associated with the body. "Neither soul nor body, and both one and the other" (p. 6), the specter bypasses materiality and its putative opposite. To elaborate these points, Derrida draws on the paradoxical dimension of Marx's invocation of the specter in the "Communist Manifesto," that most "real and concrete" of Marx's writings, which simultaneously issues from a historically specific location and is a world traveler in history. As a written text, it is rivaled only by the Bible as a force in history; yet it also quickly made itself obsolete even by Marx and Engels's own account. Written in a specific time and place, and replete with references revealing that specificity, it takes on a transcendent and universal life only through readings that are themselves historically contingent and culturally local/located.

In opening the "Manifesto" with the specter as a figure of power and agency, Derrida argues, Marx invokes "this first paternal character, as powerful as it is unreal, a hallucination or simulacrum more actual than what is blithely called a living presence" (p. 13). The specter, supernatural yet potent in the real world, operates in the opening paragraph of the "Manifesto" as the vehicle for the great project that is unifying modern Europe: "All the Powers of old Europe have entered into a holy alliance to exorcize this specter: Pope and Czar, Met-

ternich and Guizot, French Radicals and German police-spies."[6] This
ghost of the future, this incontestably immaterial figure, has also pre-
cipitated one of the mightiest alliances of modern European history.
Thus, argues Derrida, the opening of the "Manifesto" reveals the non-
viability of the tangible materialism that will be the leitmotif of the
"Manifesto." This is the tension that Derrida exploits in Marx's work:
Marxist materialism is haunted (and undone) by the specter with
which Marx commences, the specter that Marx himself has conjured
but also seeks (fruitlessly) to exorcise.

What Derrida terms the "spectral asymmetry" of the specter—its
felt but unseen presence, our incapacity to see what looks at us—disrupts all conventional specularity; it thus also wreaks havoc with the
epistemology of empiricism, particularly with empirical accounts of
power (pp. 6–7). Spectral asymmetry is achieved both through what
Derrida calls the "visor effect" of the specter—seeing without being
seen—and through what he calls the "commerce of specters," the multiple and inconstant character of their appearance. Because of this
asymmetry, the power of the specter is not empirically observable, but
it is no less tangible for being invisible—we feel the force of the look.
Thus, in a historical dimension, the dead and the not-yet-born inter-
mittently press their constraints or demands with an unmistakable
but invisible power, a power that also exceeds our conventional formulations of agency. This challenge to specularity, to both the tangi-
bility of power and to the reciprocity of visibility between actor and
acted upon, disrupts empirical and systematic efforts to apprehend
both power and history, and especially the power of the historical
in the present. While "haunting is historical . . . it is not dated, it is
never docilely given a date in the chain of presents. . . . Untimely, it
does not come to, it does not happen to, it does not befall, one day,
Europe" (p. 4).

What Derrida terms a "hauntology," which analyzes the work of
the specter in history and in history making, harbors both an eschatol-
ogy and a teleology—but "incomprehensibly": that is, in a manner
that does not add up to a comprehensive account of history's relationship to the present. The specter reverses the usual understanding of
history as origin (and the present as the teleological fruit of the origin)
by virtue of its always being a revenant, a coming back. The specter

begins by coming back, by repeating itself, by recurring in the present. It is not traceable to an origin nor to a founding event, it does not have an objective or "comprehensive" history, yet it operates as a *force*. Moreover, Derrida insists, we cannot control the comings and goings of specters, because they are by nature "furtive and untimely"; they "upset time," just as justice must entail an upsetting of the present, a referral of the present back toward our ancestors and forward toward the unborn. Hence, Derrida characterizes the politics of spectral consciousness as a "being-with" specters that is also an insurgent "politics of memory, inheritance, generations" (p. xix). To have this consciousness is to live actively with—indeed, to activate politically—the spirits of the past and the future, the bearable and unbearable memories of the past and the weight of obligation toward the unborn. By insisting on the political face of history as a persistent question about the way the past is remembered or disavowed, Derrida has rendered impossible (as does Benjamin) any pure categories in the attempt to separate history from memory. We inherit not "what really happened" to the dead but what lives on from that happening, what is conjured from it, how past generations and events occupy the force fields of the present, how they claim us, and how they haunt, plague, and inspirit our imaginations and visions for the future.

. . . .

Thus far, I have emphasized Derrida's engagement with the figure of the specter to recast the relation of past, present, and future, thereby disrupting linear time, progressive time, causal time, predictive time, and hence the very periodicity that a division into past, present, and future requires. Yet such a division is not therefore abolished. To the contrary, the figure of the specter underscores the weightiness of the relation among the three terms, marking the unbidden imposition of parts of the past on the present. It indicates the way in which the future is always already populated with certain possibilities derived from the past; the way in which it is constrained, circumscribed, inscribed by the past; the way in which it is haunted before we make and enter it. This formulation of the past's heavy yet indeterminate appearance in present and future time does not simply give us a new historical determinism, potent without being mappable or predictable. Rather, it enables a novel kind of agency with regard to the place of history in the present, an agency signaled by the notion of "conjuration."

While ghosts are "furtive and untimely," coming and going as they please, they can also be conjured and exorcised—solicited, beckoned, invoked, dismissed—and thus made to live in the present or leave the present in a manner that shapes both possibilities for and constraints on the future. Conjuring, always a mixture of conscious and unconscious elements, is also a precise and deliberate activity paradoxically combined with pure hope. We conjure the not-yet-true—for example, the dead as reborn, or an imagined triumph—in an effort to make it true. *Conjuration* is the term through which Derrida reads not only Marx's own rendering of French revolutionaries in Roman garb but also Marx's formulation (drawn in part from Shakespeare's *Timon of Athens*) in the *Economic and Philosophic Manuscripts of 1844* of the transmutation of paper into gold and of gold into personal, social, and political power (p. 45). Conjuring is also what political actors do with specters they must defeat: we conjure away certain historical haunts just as we conjure forth others. Historiography as hauntology is thus more than a new mode of figuring the presence of the past, the ineffable and unconquerable force of the past; it also opens the stage for battling with the past over possibilities for the future. In figuring the past as "alive" in the present, conjuring indexes a certain capacity to invoke and diminish it, to demand its presence on stage or to attempt to banish it to the wings. Of course, conjuration is never only or fully in our hands; but neither is it in the hands of God, historical facticity, or metaphysical axioms.

A characterization of the past as haunting the present and as conjurable in the present challenges not simply linear but progressive history. In Derrida's reformulation, history emerges as that which shadows and constrains, incites or thwarts, rather than that which moves, directs, or unfolds. History as a ghostly phenomenon does not march forward—it doesn't even march. Rather, it comes and goes, appears and recedes, materializes and evaporates, makes and gives up its claims. And it changes shape: that is, the same event or formation does not haunt in the same way across time and space. The notion of progress as the unfolding of the future is also undone by Derrida's image of political life as a stage on which specters of past and future at times appear unbidden and at other times are expressly conjured by those vying for particular futures vis-à-vis particular interpretations of the past or particular claims of homage to the past.

But Derrida's work with the specter is not intended only, and perhaps not intended at all, as a general historiography. Rather, it is a historically specific and historically remedial move. Recall that Derrida begins this work by affirming the specter as what arises at the end of something, at the moment of death or loss. The specter as a figure for history thus is linked to Derrida's diagnosis of our time both as haunted by the end of history and as a time itself "out of joint," at odds with itself, internally asunder. Each of these postulations is considered separately below.

"After the end of history, the spirit comes by *coming back* [*revenant*], it figures both a dead man who comes back and a ghost whose expected return repeats itself, again and again" (p. 10). The moment when history ends is also the moment when we are ghosted by history, by that which we no longer believe in, because what has really ended is a certain concept of history—a concept by which we continue to be haunted (p. 15). The inevitability of a fundamental concept's ghosted return following its exhaustion is part of what Derrida calls the logic of haunting, according to which the present is haunted not simply by what transpired in the past but also by what was confused or misnamed in the past, what remains unclear in meaning. To be haunted is at once to experience the profundity or significance of something from the past and not to know what that something was. When we say, "I'm not sure why, but I am haunted by what she said to me yesterday," we affirm that haunting occurs at the point of uncertainty about the meaning of an event, an utterance, a gesture. The phenomenon remains alive, refusing to recede into the past, precisely to the extent that its meaning is open and ambiguous, to the extent that it remains interpreted and contested by the present, and to the extent that it disturbs settled meanings in the present. To be haunted by something is to feel ourselves disquieted or disoriented by it, even if we cannot name or conquer its challenge. The logic of haunting is thus a logic in which there is permanent open-endedness of meaning and limits of mastery. Paradoxically, these features of haunting will turn out to constitute the site of intellectual and political agency within "hauntology."

Haunting is also unsettling to the very degree that a past remark or event or figure hovers over the present, thereby undoing the line between past and present. To be haunted often entails being touched or suffused by something that one cannot quite recall, feeling the importance of something that one has laid aside or tried to forget. It is to recognize that there is something from the past occupying the present, something whose shape or meaning eludes us. So haunting takes place between history and memory; it is simultaneously an achievement of memory and a failure of memory with regard to some significant historical effect. As an achievement, haunting keeps the phenomenon alive and potent; as a failure, it indicates or points toward a history that it cannot fully conjure or command. Disavowed, the haunting will undo the present as it works according to its own logic; yet when avowed, it does not make perfectly clear what its meaning and effects are. This is the conundrum set for us when we affirm hauntology as historiography.

To understand Derrida's diagnostic point about the "out-of-jointness" of the present, we turn to his invocation of Hamlet's time as one that parallels our own. *"The time is out of joint."* Derrida reads, rereads, and overreads this line from *Hamlet* to enable it to converge with the promise of a reformulated temporality for justice heralded by spectrality. He queries whether the remark invokes time in the sense of "*le temps* itself, the temporality of time, or else what temporality makes possible (time as *histoire*, the way things are at a certain time . . .), or else, consequently, the *monde*, the world[,] . . . our world today, our today, currentness itself" (p. 18), and then works with the possibility that it invokes time in all three senses. He exploits the diverse French translations of Shakespeare's phrase—a time that is off its hinges, broken down, out of sorts, upside down, askew—to reflect on the different dimensions of temporality and decenteredness that the phrase elicits. Derrida is especially drawn to Gide's translation, "cette epoque est déshonorée" (this age is dishonored), because it combines a strong ethical and political meaning—moral decadence, corruption of the polity, dissolution or perversion of customs—with the more general observation that things are not going as they ought to go (p. 19). It is this condition of being internally broken apart (disjointed) in the sense of being in disharmony with our own values, or off-center with regard to our own principles and institutions, that Derrida seizes on as the diagnostic moment connecting Shakespeare with Marx with his own reading of the injustice of our own time. This moment, Derrida insists, calls for a different order of justice, a justice that breaks with the current order of things even as it marks continuity between past, present, and future. But what Derrida calls the out-of-jointness of time is crucially distinguished from a notion of a time in "crisis." The former indicates a more subtly corrosive condition than the latter; it suggests a time that is wearing badly: a time whose languages have grown thin or hypocritical, whose practices have grown hollow, whose ideals are neither realized nor perhaps any longer suited to the age.

What conventionally sets time right again is the law; but in Derrida's account, law's traditional connection with vengeance, and even with blood revenge, can do no more than perpetuate the out-of-jointness of the times, because it addresses only its symptoms. (This claim would seem to be corroborated by the boundless litigiousness of the present age, and especially by the conversion of historical-political claims of oppression to legal claims for rights or reparations.) Justice cast in legal terms repeats the fundamental principles and practices of the current order of justice and thus condemns us to the out-of-jointness of our time. A formulation of justice intended to rectify that disjointedness must rely on something other than the law; for Derrida, it must be beyond right, debt, calculation, and vengeance—"Otherwise justice risks being reduced once again to juridical-moral rules, norms, or representations, within an inevitable totalizing horizon" (p. 28). Derrida seeks a noncontemporaneous idiom for justice, one that embraces out-of-jointness as itself the spur to justice and as the mode of a de-totalized condition of justice. A de-totalized justice is necessarily in a state of what Derrida calls "disjointure": it is reconciled to the endless commerce of specters, and to the indeterminacy of the past and of the past's relationship to the present. It challenges us to craft justice from the material of the specters of the past and present, honoring the dead and attending to the not-yet-born—and all this with minimal reliance on imagined metaphysical or epistemological foundations.

In this admittedly partial and self-serving reading of Marx, Derrida makes deconstruction not only compatible with but something of a necessary heir to Marx.[7] His reading of Marx, so patently against the grain, highlights the ghosts that Derrida knows Marx disclaimed— "Marx does not like ghosts . . . he does not want to believe in them. But he thinks of nothing else" (pp. 46–47). As a study of Marx, this reading converges with the one I have offered in chapter 4 as it points to the immateriality that haunts Marx's materialism, the spirit that haunts his empiricism, the alchemical magic that haunts his secular realism. But Derrida offers as well the tentative beginnings of a historiography for historical-political consciousness in the time after progress. He offers strategies for developing historical consciousness that rely neither on a progressive historiography nor on historical determinism more generally, strategies for conceiving our relation to past and future that coin responsibility and possibilities for action out of indeterminacy. It is a permanently contestable historiography, one that makes contestable histories an overt feature of our political life as it encourages us to struggle for and against particular conjurations of the past. It never claims to exhaust or settle historical questions. History becomes less what we dwell in, are propelled by, or are determined by than what we fight over, fight for, and aspire to honor in our practices of justice.

BENJAMIN'S "THESES ON THE PHILOSOPHY OF HISTORY"

> Thinking involves not only the flow of thoughts, but their arrest as well. Where thinking suddenly stops in a configuration pregnant with tensions, it gives that configuration a shock, by which it crystallizes into a monad. A historical materialist approaches a historical subject only where he encounters it as a monad. In this structure he recognizes the sign of a Messianic cessation of happening, or, put differently, a revolutionary chance in the fight for the oppressed past. He takes cognizance of it in order to blast a specific era out of the homogeneous course of history—blasting a specific life out of the era

> or a specific work out of the lifework. As a result of this
> method the lifework is preserved in this work and at the same
> time canceled; in the lifework the era; and in the era, the en-
> tire course of history. The nourishing fruit of the historically
> understood contains time as a precious but tasteless seed.
> —Walter Benjamin, "Theses on the Philosophy of History"

For Walter Benjamin, the conundrum of modern history is its stormy forward movement absent a telos. But the conundrum of radical political action (set against Marx historiographically, while joining with him politically) lies in the need to break this stream of history, to interrupt or arrest historical process in order to inaugurate another possibility or, to use the term Benjamin was so fond of, "actuality" (*Aktualität*). The German word connotes both a realization or actualization (of possibility) and a making present, a materialization, even a particular production of the present through what is actualized in it. In Benjamin's deployment of *Aktualität*, that which is realized is simultaneously grasped as invented and inventive.[8] Thus, what Marx, after Hegel, called world-historical events do not for Benjamin fulfill or even chart history's mission: instead they explode historical processes, reroute history, even begin it anew by "actualizing" some element of the past as possibility in the present.

In his critical engagement with the notion of progress, on which he considered all modern strains of philosophy and political life to rest, Benjamin by no means simply rejects historical process or historical force. To the contrary, the backward-looking angel of history both sees and feels the terrible press of history—a "single catastrophe which keeps piling wreckage upon wreckage," a storm that "has got caught in his wings with such violence that he can no longer close them"— but can do nothing to stop it.[9] Indeed, it is the task not of the angel but of an ill-defined "us" to interrupt this force, to seize moments in the present as possibilities for action. Thus, Benjamin argues, "the awareness that they are about to make the continuum of history explode is characteristic of the revolutionary classes at the moment of their action" (p. 261). Great revolutions, he insists, always introduce new calendars, thereby marking both the interruption of one trajectory of history and the inauguration of another—an interruption and transformation of the very temporality of politics, an interruption and transformation that historicists can never grasp.

Benjamin seeks to cast "interruption" as the spirit and metaphor not only of revolutionary politics but also of everyday politics. Interruption or "blasting open the continuum of history" becomes a kind of persistent revolutionary political orientation that breaks both with the notion of progress and with its cousin, uniquely "ripe" revolutionary conditions, even as it attends closely to historical configurations of opportunity or possibility. The "arrest" of history that revolution achieves not only sets history's sails in a new direction (as opposed to the progressivist view that revolution is a teleological conclusion of a historical process) but also indicts a fundamental premise of progress, namely that more just and felicitous times have steadily displaced more impoverished ones. For Benjamin, the past is not an inferior version of the present but an exploitable cache of both traumatic and utopian scenes. Thus, the theological moment that Benjamin believes inheres in all revolutionary hopes pertains to traces of the good life left behind, preserved and cultivated as imagistic memories. These are the traces that would inspirit revolutionary action, and it is precisely the ideology of progress that eliminates them from view. What Benjamin terms the revolutionary-historical "tiger's leap into the past" is thus the grand revolutionary gesture—at once political and intellectual—of disinterring repressed emancipatory hopes and experiences from their tombs beneath the putative march of progress. In Lutz Niethammer's phrase: "Benjamin's hope is that . . . it will be possible . . . to bring time to a halt . . . and to reach beyond the most insupportable conditions to assist the species-recollection of the good life . . . as the guide to human action. Through his tiger leaps, the historian must stand at their side and blast the repressed hopes out of the progress-leveled past."[10]

This "tiger's leap" is a complicated one, however, for as Benjamin notes, "it takes place in an arena where the ruling class gives the commands" (p. 261); the trick is to seize the interruption of history from the maw of bourgeois co-optation. When Benjamin adds that "the same leap in the open air of history is the dialectical one, which is how Marx understood the revolution" (p. 261), he is identifying the struggle between revolutionary and bourgeois forces as a struggle over the present as well as over the meanings of history. History interrupted is a fecund political moment but it comes with no guarantees, with no lack of struggle and no certainty about the outcome. That is why Benjamin refers to this moment only as "a revolutionary *chance* in the fight for the oppressed past" (p. 263, emphasis added).

But how paradoxical is the notion of historicized political consciousness poised for action that Benjamin develops! Deeply attuned to the possibilities that history presents and that can be created within history, it is also committed to a kind of "forgetting" in which history is not simply blasted apart but is "gaily parted with."[11] Thus, the historical memory that Benjamin cultivates as political possibility in one moment is literally exploded by revolutionary action in another. History is never merely realized by revolutionary action but is invented, reworked, and also destroyed by it. Thus the history that Benjamin cherishes as resource for political action is also the history that must be treated indifferently, as dispensable, without reverence.

For a clearer view of this paradox, and its importance in developing a politics "after history" that also draws its energies from historical consciousness, we return to Benjamin's enigmatic angel. The figure of the angel in Benjamin's ninth thesis on the philosophy of history carries (but does not exhaust) his critique of progress and thus contributes to a reframing of the problem of political knowledge and political action in the era of *posthistoire*.[12] Gershom Scholem's genealogy of Benjamin's crafting of this figure (from Klee's *Angelus Novus*, which Benjamin owned, as well as from other sources) is immensely helpful in this regard, as is Niethammer's reading of the ninth thesis. Scholem begins by noting that the Hebrew *mal'āk*, which "angel" (in Greek, *angelos*) translates, also means "messenger." He adds that in one strain of Jewish tradition, each of us is thought to have a personal angel that represents our secret self, albeit in a problematic way: this angel can enter into opposition to and tension with the human to whom it is attached.[13] So Benjamin's messenger of history, harboring history's secret meaning, immediately casts history as tragic: unknowable to itself and in tension with itself, history is propelled toward a future to which its back is turned and which carries meaning only as a witness to catastrophe. The secret truth of history is at best a negative one, centered on this nebulously defined catastrophe; but perhaps more important, history's "secret" is that its movement has no inherent meaning at all. The messenger of history is also paradoxically mute: it cannot speak to the future, even as history is implicated in the future. That is, history has bearing on the future insofar as the storm from Paradise is blowing toward the future (p. 261). But the angel cannot look there, it cannot speak, nor can it intervene in the storm into which it is only and always blown backward. The muteness and the impotence of the backward body—neither eyes nor hands can come to terms with where it is going, neither are of any use in grasping or shaping the body's experience—together figure the agency of the meaning of history as approximately nothing.

Paradise, Scholem suggests in this reading of Benjamin, is the primal past of humanity as well the utopian image of our future redemption; Benjamin borrows from Karl Krause a figure of Paradise as both origin and goal.[14] But the storm prevents the angel—history's meaning—from the redemptive work suggested here. The angel cannot "stay, awaken the dead, and make whole what has been smashed" (p. 257), which Benjamin claims as its yearning, because there is a forward (nonprogressive) press of history, and because the angel is powerless and speechless. The angel is pushed toward a future into which it does not gaze, cannot gaze, but cannot not go, and also looks out over a past that it cannot redeem even as it longs to do so. The angel, however, sees history for what it is: "one single catastrophe," the ruins of freedom unrealized.

Lutz Niethammer also approaches Benjamin's angel theologically but from a different angle. Why, Niethammer asks, does Benjamin give us the image of an *angel* of history, when, on the one hand, historians usually choose a muse as their higher being and, on the other, angels in the Bible and in the Jewish tradition more generally relate to God or humanity, but not to history, which they typically hover outside of or above? What the Hebrew Bible knows, Niethammer argues, is the past, and this knowledge "is typically denoted by the same word that refers to what the face is turned towards in attention; while the word for the future also signifies what is hidden behind one's back." So, Niethammer concludes, "the position and line of vision of the new (or still young) angel in the storm thus evoke the religious tradition, as does the storm itself."[15] The religious line of vision of the angel is thus precisely at odds with the secular dynamic of progress and reason constitutive of the Enlightenment. It is a vision that draws on its knowledge of Paradise—again, both an archaic and a utopian knowledge—or on the hopes and dreams of humankind. But disenchantment, itself occasioned by the idealization of progress and rationality, drains the power from this tradition's insights and instigations—indeed overwhelms them as if by a storm, a storm that makes ruins of everything, including messianic hopes and dreams. Benjamin's angel would seem to signify the extent to which the tradition of religious redemption (and hence religious inspiration) is rendered impotent by the force of ideological secularism: "the victims [of the history of progress] no longer have access to the power of religious redemption; for in the raging wind of disenchantment the angel is driven up and away."[16] Under the hegemony of progress, the divine messenger is incapable of action and redemptive politics is impossible. Only the rupture of progressive ideology, the "arrest" of historical process, permits an opening through which the politically productive elements of theology can return to history, allowing the redemptive powers of hope, dream, and utopian passion a place on the political and historical stage. Only then can history be rewritten, as a different future is coined from the present. But this description also suggests that the rupture of history and progressive ideology constitutes a simultaneously theological and secular opening for political understanding and action. It is an opening for both the messianic dreams *and* the human crafting that are erased by progressive historiography and politics. Thus does postfoundationalism potentially become at once spiritual and historical: its challenge to historical automatism reactivates the figures banished by that automatism—conscious and unconscious memories, hopes, and longings.

Taken together, Scholem's and Niethammer's readings suggest that while progress may be a delusion, it has functioned as a powerful ideology that has both displaced the Edenic elements of the past and destroyed the very memory of their existence. With the force of a storm, "piling wreckage upon wreckage," it has rendered theological yearnings impotent on earth. The angel who represents these yearnings and who apprehends the limitations of an Enlightenment perspective sees the ruin of this course of history; but powerless to express its insight, the angel is itself a passive wisp in the winds of history. Yet this melancholy figure does not imply that Benjamin abandons the project of redemption and revolution. Instead, Benjamin's reformulated dialectical materialism, far too heavy with messianic and literary tropes to be acceptable to most Marxists, poses the prospect of simultaneously interrupting the continuum of history and redeeming the past.

Revolution and redemption at once and achieved through one another—it is hardly the most immediately plausible moment of hope to issue from Benjamin's despairing vision. To increase its credibility, we must leave the ninth thesis and investigate further both Benjamin's critique of progress and his formulation of dialectics. In the thirteenth thesis, Benjamin offers a terse, threefold critique of the conception of progress presented in the social democratic theory of his milieu. The Social Democrats, he claims, understand progress as "first of all, the progress of mankind itself[;] . . . [s]econdly, . . . something boundless, in keeping with the infinite perfectibility of mankind[;] . . . [and t]hirdly, . . . irresistible, something that automatically pursued a straight or spiral course" (p. 260). "Each of these predicates," he remarks, "is controversial and open to criticism." Yet Benjamin's critique goes beyond simply pointing out the groundlessness of the various premises of progress and instead aims at what "they have in common. The concept of the historical progress of mankind cannot be sundered from the concept of its progression through a homogeneous, empty time. A critique of the concept of such a progression must be the basis of any criticism of the concept of progress itself" (pp. 260–61).

What Benjamin names "homogeneous, empty time" is precisely the opposite of historical time. Time, he insists, is always "filled by the presence of the Now" (p. 261); time always has particular content that itself renders a particular meaning of time, rather than the other way around. Time has no transcendental status outside of the particular present ("the time of the now") that invests it with questions, meaning, or projects. Thus, the fundamental trouble with all notions of historical progress is their imbrication with a false transcendentalism—progress inevitably transpires above human consciousness, activity, and concerns. Within a progressive metanarrative, time is unstructured by anything other than progress, and historical memory or consciousness framed by this metanarrative imagines itself to be unstructured by the present, and hence unsituated and unsaturated by the present. Benjamin's objection to progressive historiography is therefore not simply its groundlessness as historiography but the havoc it wreaks with a historically oriented political consciousness. Rather than focusing this consciousness on the parameters of the present, rather than engaging it to evoke and create historical memory, progress lifts consciousness out of time and space, treating past, present, and their relation as givens.

The problem of developing a political consciousness oriented toward historically shaped possibility is further illuminated in the eighth thesis, which immediately precedes Benjamin's invocation of the angel of history.

> The tradition of the oppressed teaches us that the "state of emergency" in which we live is not the exception but the rule. We must attain to a conception of history that is in keeping with this insight. Then we shall clearly realize that it is our task to bring about a real state of emergency, and this will improve our position in the struggle against Fascism. One reason why Fascism has a chance is that in the name of progress its opponents treat it as a historical norm. The current amazement that the things we are experiencing are "still" possible in the twentieth century is *not* philosophical. This amazement is not the beginning of knowledge—unless it is the knowledge that the view of history which gives rise to it is untenable. (p. 257)

Like Derrida, Benjamin insists that it is not history that "ends" in the twentieth century but a certain concept of history, a concept that nonetheless continues to grip political thinking and reaction even in its ghostly form, producing "amazement" and literal dumbfounding. He sees progress, so often understood by radicals and reformers as a wellspring of political hope, as functioning in just the opposite way. Progress reconciles and attaches its adherents to an inevitable (even fatalistic) and unwittingly normative account of political formations and events. The hopefulness that a progressive view of history offers is both delusional and ultimately conservative, precluding a politics devoted to bringing about a "state of emergency" that can break with this present or "blast open the continuum of history" (p. 262). More-over, Benjamin argues, while it is the downtrodden who often cling hardest to the progressive promise, progress always measures the con-dition of the dominant class and is part of the ideology that naturalizes its dominance.[17] A progressive historiography ratifies the dominance of the bourgeoisie by tacitly articulating an ideology that erases the condition of the defeated or the oppressed in the name of a historical automatism, that is, in a process with no agent, no powers, and, most important, no victims—or at least none for whom anyone or anything is accountable.

It is this seamless historical narrative of "empty time"—reinforced by one version of dialectical materialism but challenged by Benjamin's version—that Benjamin seeks to disrupt with alternative historical im-ages and new sites of political possibility.

> Historical materialism has to abandon the epic element in history. It blasts the epoch out of the reified "continuity of history." But it also blasts open the homogeneity of the epoch. It saturates it with *ecrasite*, that is, the present. . . .
>
> The destructive or critical impetus in materialist historiography comes into play in that blasting apart of historical continuity which allows the historical object to constitute itself. . . . Materialist histori-ography does not choose its objects casually. It does not pluck them from the process of history, but rather blasts them out of it. Its pre-cautions are more extensive, its occurrences more essential.[18]

The "blasting open" or "blasting apart" that Benjamin identifies as the work of the historical materialist is neither objectively arrived at nor randomly crafted. It is instead a very specific kind of interpretive work, one that affirms historical contingency in its vision, acknowledges the element of invention resulting from this contingent quality, and yet insists on the materiality of the past that it glimpses and renders in the present. It insists, in other words, on the material unfolding of the past, but distinguishes this material unfolding from the bearing of the past on the present, and from our grasp of the past in the present.

In the sixth thesis, Benjamin declares: "To articulate the past histori-cally does not mean to recognize it 'the way it really was' (Ranke). It means to seize hold of a memory as it flashes up at a moment of danger" (p. 255). This formulation of the history of the present as fleeting, appearing in fiery but transitory images, and as both capturing and signaling a moment of danger (the danger of being colonized, of rendering both interpreter and the past what Benjamin calls "a tool of the ruling classes") recurs several times in Benjamin; it corresponds directly to the project of using historical memory to undo the inevitability or the givenness of the present. The blasting that Benjamin invokes both illuminates and forces open possibilities in the present, in what Benjamin called "this particular Now," possibilities that are then "actualized." The "possible" in Benjamin, is, according to Irving Wohlfarth, paradoxically "both a measure and a gift"—a measure of the contours and contents of the present, but also a gift to the would-be revolutionary who wishes to make a different present. "True actuality," Wohlfarth adds, is untimely yet historically located—it stands both "in" and "against" its time, and thus actuality "must be 'wooed' from unfruitful surfaces."[19] What Benjamin calls "the truly actual" are intimations of another reality that can be actualized or realized only through political transformation; they lodge in "the oddest and most crabbed phenomena" yet "point from the heart of the present beyond itself." Again, revolutionary possibility does not simply ripen once and for all but rather takes specific shape in a specific time and is given this shape, at least in part, by revolutionary actors and historians. "Actuality, thus conceived, is a matter of actualizing the specific potential of this particular now."[20]

At this point, we are prepared to understand another of Benjamin's insistent connections between revolutionary historical consciousness and theological work. In appendix A of the "Theses on the Philosophy of History," he writes:

> Historicism contents itself with establishing a causal connection between various moments in history. But no fact that is a cause is for that very reason historical. It became historical posthumously, as it were, through events that may be separated from it by thousands of years. A historian who takes this as his point of departure stops telling the sequence of events like the beads of a rosary. Instead, he grasps the constellation which his own era has formed with a definite

earlier one. Thus he establishes a conception of the present as the "time of the now" which is shot through with chips of Messianic time. (p. 263)

Grasping the constellation that our own era forms with an earlier one entails grasping the extent to which (selected elements of the) past and present ignite each other, resemble each other, articulate with one another, figure meaning in one another. This grasp allows the past to illuminate the possibilities of the present, and especially to open hope in the present. Such an opening in turn allows the present itself to emerge as a time in which redemption—that is, the connection of a particular political aim in the present with a particular formation of oppression in the past—might be possible. This articulation of past and present constitutes those "chips of Messianic time" that redeem history not all at once but rather in fragments and patches. Benjamin's reformulated dialectical materialism abandons the totalized project of nineteenth-century dialectics, even as it refuses to abandon that project's redemptive aim.

Consider again those elements of modern historiography that Benjamin criticizes. "Historicism," "empty time," "eternity"—these are Benjamin's pejorative names for conceptions of history that misrepresent both the powers constitutive of the past and the possibilities of opening a different future. But more than misrepresentations, they are also sites of political corruption or disorientation, sometimes dangerous ones. Recall Benjamin's claim that "nothing has corrupted the German working class so much as the notion that it was moving with the current," a current Benjamin names "empty time" because it is divorced from "this particular Now," the diverse elements that constitute a present that might be other than itself (p. 258). As Derrida does in emphasizing the spectral nature of Marxist historiography, Benjamin here claims to be offering a way of reading and enacting Marx rather than departing from him. The dialectics that Benjamin takes over and radically reworks from Marxism does not signify the process by which history moves; instead, it aims to capture a peculiar meeting of past and present that occurs in the *image* of the past as a "blazing up." In *The Arcades Project*, he attempts to explain why:

It isn't that the past casts its light on the present or the present casts
its light on the past: rather, an image is that in which the *Then* and
the *Now* come into a constellation like a flash of lightning. In other
words: image is dialectics at a standstill. For while the relation of the
present to the past is a purely temporal, continuous one, the relation
of the Then to the Now is dialectical—not development but image,
leaping forth. Only dialectical images are genuine images; and the
place one happens upon them is language.[21]

For Benjamin, dialectics defines the transformation achieved by the
encounter of past and present, and images are the frozen expression
of this encounter. In what he sometimes calls "true historical materialism," Benjamin claims that "history breaks down into images, not
stories":[22] this very transduction of images for stories constitutes the
immanent critique of the concept of progress that Benjamin insists is
levied by "true" dialectical materialism, a critique waged *against* other
versions of dialectical materialism. Benjamin's materialism entails an
appreciation of the empirical truth of the past, but dialectics complicates this truth by recognizing that the past's play in the present is
selective, interpreted, and imagistic. Similarly, while Benjamin's dialectical materialism converges with what Marxists call material conditions of actions, it distinguishes these conditions from the particular
way in which the past presses on the present. He is thus differentiating
three elements frequently collapsed by Marxists into one: the materialism of the past (a question of what happened), the materialism of the
present (a question of what historical conditions shape contemporary
political possibility), and the way in which past and present take their
shape from one another in contemporary political consciousness (a
question of memory and consciousness). In Benjamin's rendering, dialectics functions as a name for the process by which some element of
the past is made to live in the present, is ignited by the present, and
transforms present and past in this illumination. The past can have
occurred without memory but it cannot live in the present without
memory; significantly, historical memory is conveyed imagistically
even when it is carried by narrative. Benjamin makes this claim with
particular sharpness in response to a reprimand from Max Horkheimer. Horkheimer argues that "the assertion of [the] incompleteness

[of history] is idealistic, if completeness isn't included in it. Past injustice has occurred and is done with. The murdered are really murdered. . . . If one takes incompleteness completely seriously, one has to believe in the Last Judgment. . . . Perhaps there's a difference with regard to incompleteness between the positive and the negative, such that only injustice, terror, and the pain of the past are irreparable." Benjamin responds:

> The corrective to this line of thought lies in the reflection that history is not just a science but also a form of memoration. (*Eine Form des Eingedenkens*). What science has "established," memoration can modify. Memoration can make the incomplete (happiness) into something complete, and the complete (suffering) into something incomplete. That is theology; but in memoration we discover the experience (*Erfahrung*) that forbids us to conceive of history as thoroughly a-theological, even though we barely dare not attempt to write it according to literally theological concepts.[23]

Like Derrida's conception of history as haunting the present, history as images can never add up to a coherent totality but rather is always "incomplete." Dialectical images evoke slices of the past that bear on the present, that "blaze up" in the present, and that potentially tear up the conventional conception and relation of present and past. Derrida and Benjamin share this rejection of historical totalization in favor of a fragmented and fragmentary historiography and both, somewhat perversely, act in the name of Marx. Indeed, Benjamin is unapologetic about his insistence on the imagistic dimension of historical recognition—its truth value pertains precisely to its transitory, partial, and contingent character, its disruption of settled stories. In his notes on method in *The Arcades Project*, he says he wishes to demonstrate "that the materialistic presentation of history is imagistic in a higher sense than traditional historiography."[24] And he insists that the materialistic presentation of history is paradoxically more attuned to the Real to the extent that it cultivates the expression of the connection of past to present in an image, which is the medium of individual and collective memory and experience.

While this emphasis on the conjuring of historical images places dialectics in a register far more subjective than that of Marx, it is subjectivity of a very particular sort. We have already seen that dialectics, for Benjamin, does not represent an objective process of development in the world, but rather is a name for the play of history in the present, the play between present and past in a particular political moment, a play that transforms past and present into the "Then" and "Now" as a form of mutual illumination. Heavily dependent on memory, this play is also fueled by anxiety about certain losses in the past and about losing position in the present, and hence by anxiety about the capacity to make a future. But though imagistic history is subjective, it is important to note that the form of this subjectivism is not individual. History does not simply draw on memory but produces it (and thereby, Benjamin adds, also presumes "destruction"); this is the phenomenon that places the past in a "critical condition" by attending to those "jags and crags that offer a handhold to someone who wishes to move beyond them."[25] Here, we are inevitably reminded of Foucault's genealogies, which are intended, *inter alia*, to articulate political possibilities in the present by telling alternative histories of the present and by producing a historical ontology of the present—one that reveals the fissures and breaks in its production, thereby interrupting a seamless narrative of the past that yielded a seamless architecture of the present. By featuring memory as something produced rather than given, by activating it as a strategic force that is engaged in "the fight for the oppressed past," by being instructed in it and cultivating its possibilities, we open "the strait gate through which the Messiah might enter" (p. 264).[26] Redemption of past suffering and retrieval of past possibility both become possible in the project of forging a future.

· · · ·

We are now in a position to link Benjamin's cultivation of historical memory to disrupt the givenness of the present with his political critique of a melancholic relationship to the political present. Benjamin seeks to discern a way in which lost moments in the past, rather than being treated as lamentable and unrecoverable on the one hand or as superseded by progress on the other, might be cultivated as *incitations* in the present. What Benjamin tendentiously names "left melancholia" is a condition produced by attachment to a notion of progress in which opportunities missed or political formations lost are experienced as permanent and unrecoverable. Left melancholia thus represents a refusal to come to terms with the particular character of the present: it is a failure to understand history other than as "empty time" or progress. It signifies as well a certain narcissism with regard to one's past political attachments and identity that frames all contemporary investments in political mobilization, alliance, or transformation.[27] If, however, history does not move toward a goal, if it does not unfold according to a plan, then, as Wohlfarth explains, "every historical moment has its own revolutionary chance—including, therefore, those moments where possibilities are severely reduced."[28]

The irony of melancholia, of course, is that attachment to the object of one's sorrowful loss supersedes the desire to recover from this loss, to live free of it in the present, to be unburdened by it. This supersession is what renders melancholia a persistent condition, a state, indeed a full-blown structure of desire, rather than a transient response to death or loss. In his 1917 meditation on melancholia, Freud reminds us of a second singular feature of melancholy: it entails "a loss of a more ideal kind [than mourning]. The object has not perhaps actually died, but has been lost as an object of love."[29] Moreover, Freud suggests, the melancholic often will not know precisely what it is about the object that has been loved and lost—"this would suggest that melancholia is in some way related to an object-loss which is withdrawn from consciousness, in contradistinction to mourning, in which there is nothing about the loss that is unconscious."[30] The loss precipitating melancholy is more often than not unavowed and unavowable. Freud also suggests that the melancholic subject—low in self-regard, despairing, even suicidal—shifts the reproach of the once-loved object (a reproach leveled for not living up to the idealization by the beloved) onto itself, thus preserving the love or idealization of the object even as the loss of this love is experienced as melancholic.

Now why would Benjamin use the term *melancholia*, and the emotional economy it represents, to talk about a particular formation on and of the Left? Benjamin never offers a precise formulation of left melancholia. Instead, he deploys it as a term of opprobrium for those more beholden to certain long-held sentiments and objects than to the possibilities of political transformation in the present. Benjamin is particularly attuned to the melancholic's investment in "things" and in precepts or stories that acquire thinglike form. In the *Trauerspiel*, he argues that "melancholy betrays the world for the sake of knowledge," suggesting that the loyalty of the melancholic converts its truth ("every loyal vow or memory") about its beloved into a thing—indeed, imbues knowledge itself with a thinglike quality. Another version of this formulation: "in its tenacious self-absorption [melancholy] embraces dead objects in its contemplation." More simply, melancholia is loyal "to the world of things,"[31] suggesting a certain logic of fetishism—with all the conservatism and withdrawal from human relations that fetishistic desire implies—within the melancholic logic. In the critique of Erich Kastner's poems in which he first coins the phrase "left melancholia," Benjamin suggests that sentiments themselves become things for the left melancholic, who "takes as much pride in the traces of former spiritual goods as the bourgeois do in their material goods."[32] We are more loyal to our left passions and reasons, our left analyses and convictions, than to the existing world that we presumably seek to alter with these terms or to the future that would be aligned with them. Left melancholy, in short, is Benjamin's name for a mournful, conservative, backward-looking attachment to feelings, analyses, or relations that have become fetishized and frozen in the heart of the critic. And if supplementation from Freud is helpful here, then this condition presumably issues from some unaccountable loss, some unavowably crushed ideal—an ideal that lives in empty time rather than the time of the Now precisely to the extent that it is imagined to have been killed by time, that it is lost in time, that it is unrecoverable.

To "stand entirely to the left of the possible" is the political stance of the left melancholic, who prefers a particular analysis—who prefers to brood on the losses that this analysis documents—over seizing and developing the prospects of political transformation in the present. This is the stance of the "revolutionary hack" and contrasts with that of the thinker-activist, who would "stand to the left within the possible."[33] It would be a mistake to misread Benjamin's critique here as an argument for becoming reconciled to the conditions of the present or for rejecting the place of historical memory in shaping the possibili-

ties of the present. Rather, we are encountering again that most difficult paradox in Benjamin's formulation of the bearing of history on
the political present: his insistence that we must cultivate memory
while fostering a means of "gaily parting with the past."[34] We must
reconcile ourselves to parting with our past—and here Benjamin
quotes Marx and not Nietzsche—if we are to do the work of mourning
rather than submit to melancholia, the latter being the condition that
binds us to the past as a collection of things, as a way of knowing, in
such a way that we are complacent about the present. But parting with
the past does not mean forgetting it; it involves instead what Benjamin
terms "mindfulness," a particular form of remembering aimed at rendering history as what Norbert Bolz and Willem van Reijen call "an
outrage to the present." They elaborate:

> The contemporary accentuates the present as something that is his-
> torically crucial, as a crisis. History can do it justice not as a science
> but only as a "form of being mindful." Mindfulness means remem-
> brance stretched by forgetting; here, forgetting should be understood
> not as not-remembering, but as counter-remembering. In mind-
> fulness, what has been experienced is not pinned down but opened
> up to its pre- and post-history. But this also means that through mind-
> fulness past suffering is experienced as something unfinished.[35]

Suffering that is not yet finished is not only suffering that must still be
endured but also suffering that can still be redeemed; it might develop
another face through contemporary practices. Making a historical
event or formation contemporary, making it "an outrage to the present" and thus exploding or reworking both the way in which it has
been remembered and the way in which it is positioned in historical
consciousness as "past," is precisely the opposite of bringing that phenomena to "closure" through reparation or apology (our most ubiquitous form of historical political thinking today). The former demands
that we redeem the past through a specific and contemporary practice
of justice; the latter gazes impotently at the past even as it attempts to
establish history as irrelevant to the present or, at best, as a reproachful
claim or grievance in the present. Hence Benjamin's sense of history
as both an "activation of the past" and a convocation of demands on

the present, both an accusation against the present and a challenge to fixed and conventional understandings of the past. Hence, too, his insistence on the possibility of redeeming the past (and thus actually transforming the past) through revolutionary action in the present.

. . . .

The memoration that Benjamin locates at the nexus of historical understanding and political consciousness is neither an individual nor institutional nor collective memory of "what really happened"; it is, rather, a dynamic, episodic, agentic, and imagistic form of remembering that counters the force of one conjuration of the past with that of another. It is simultaneously a coming to terms with our losses and a redemption of them, achieved by cultivating a different version of them in a rearticulation of past and present. What Benjamin offers, then, is not so much a way (for historians) to do history as a way (for political actors) to think historically, a way to develop political consciousness of the historically inflected construction of contemporary political life and to discern or fashion openings or possibilities there. Benjamin also offers a way to address history as we make a future—providing not just a method of consulting the past but a means of redeeming or transforming it, and thus a way of recovering the past that paradoxically loosens its grip on our political psyches at the moment it is addressed consciously and deliberately.

Taken together, Benjamin's strange and incomplete dialectical materialism and Derrida's "hauntology" certainly will not satisfy those who want scientific, systematic, or empirically precise formulas to determine how the past bears on the present. Nor will it satisfy those buoyed by a belief that *posthistoire* means that we are without responsibility to history and are unclaimed by it—that we spring free of history into a present where we can conjure meanings and possibilities as we wish. It will not satisfy unreconstructed liberals, for whom the continued claim of progress and belief in the autonomy of the will render history largely irrelevant to political life except as episodes of trauma or greatness, episodes to recoil from or to emulate. And it will not satisfy unreconstructed Marxists, for whom history is always extremely heavy and determining, radically constraining the scope of possibilities in the present, and for whom iron laws of history reveal what the future must be. But it may offer some initial sightings for those who wish to discern a ground for political action that attends to and mobilizes history once history appears to lack a distinct shape and trajectory. This is the possibility held out by these postmaterialists who work more in language and image than in historical data, by these post-Marxists who want to extend, revive, and enliven the Marxist project with figures that Marx could not avow, even as he spawned them. Taken together, the reflections of Derrida and Benjamin tender not a new conception of historical development but novel touchstones for a political consciousness that would mobilize and activate history rather than submitting to, fulfilling, taming, or jettisoning it. It is a consciousness that simultaneously seeks to ignite the past and to open a path for departing from it, one that conjures the power of the past while resisting any preordained implications of that power for the making of a more just future. It may even be a political consciousness that offers modest new possibilities for the practice of freedom.

NOTES

CHAPTER ONE
POLITICS OUT OF HISTORY

1. That is, to paraphrase Freud, "I know the fetishized object does not really contain the unparalleled value I ascribe to it, but still I regard it as if it did."

2. For elaborations of the necessarily reactionary character of a fundamentalism developed in response to a challenge to those fundamental grounds themselves, see William Connolly, *The Ethos of Pluralization* (Minneapolis: University of Minnesota Press, 1995), especially chap. 1; and Wendy Brown, *States of Injury: Power and Freedom in Late Modernity* (Princeton: Princeton University Press, 1995), particularly chap. 2.

3. Of course, there have been thinkers in the past three centuries who did not subscribe to this cheery view of things—thinkers such as Rousseau, Nietzsche, and Benjamin. But their respective critiques of the progress narrative went hand in glove with their critiques of modernity and liberalism, thus affirming the imbrication of modernity and progress.

4. See Bob Dole's 1996 convention speech, "I Will Restore the Promise of America," *Washington Post*, August 16, 1996, sec. A, p. 36.

5. Gore Vidal, *Palimpsest: A Memoir* (New York: Penguin, 1995); and see also his historical novel *The Golden Age* (New York: Doubleday, 2000).

6. A few of the figures constituting this spectrum: Francis Fukuyama, Jacques Derrida, Fredric Jameson, Gianni Vattimo, Hayden White, Robert R. Berkhofer, Jr., Joan W. Scott, Jean Baudrillard.

7. See Scott Lash and John Urry, *The End of Organized Capitalism* (Madison: University of Wisconsin Press, 1987), pp. 5–6.

8. Karl Marx and Friedrich Engels, "The Communist Manifesto," in *The Marx-Engels Reader*, ed. Robert C. Tucker, 2nd ed. (New York: Norton, 1978), p. 474.

9. The challenge to assimilation and integration is the exclusive purview neither of cultural separatists or nationalists, nor of left or poststructuralist critics of liberalism. Consider the extent to which recent liberal political theory has been engaged by the problem of liberalism's cultural normativity and has sought to

formulate strategies of membership that at the very least supplement those of assimilation or integration. See Michael Walzer, *On Toleration* (New Haven: Yale University Press, 1997); Charles Taylor et al., *Multiculturalism: Examining the Politics of Recognition*, ed. Amy Gutmann (Princeton: Princeton University Press, 1994); Will Kymlicka, *Multicultural Citizenship: A Liberal Theory of Minority Rights* (Oxford: Clarendon Press; New York: Oxford University Press, 1995).

10. See William Connolly, *Identity/Difference: Democratic Negotiations of Political Paradox* (Ithaca, N.Y.: Cornell University Press, 1991), pp. 20–24.

11. Other movements of ethnic purity, from those in France to those in the former Yugoslavia, could be similarly interpreted.

12. A contemporary example of this recognition by non-Marxists of the variable impact of rights is provided by those advocates of hate speech regulation who regard First Amendment protections of free speech as, *inter alia*, protecting socially dominant subjects while increasing the vulnerability of subordinate subjects, thus reinforcing existing social stratification. See, e.g., Mari Matsuda et al., *Words That Wound: Critical Race Theory, Assaultive Speech, and the First Amendment* (Boulder, Colo.: Westview Press, 1993).

CHAPTER TWO
MORALISM AS ANTI-POLITICS

1. Stuart Hall, *The Hard Road to Renewal: Thatcherism and the Crisis of the Left* (London: Verso, 1988), p. 8.

2. Herbert Marcuse, *One Dimensional Man* (Boston: Beacon Press, 1964), p. xiv.

3. These questions assume that however much a left project was epistemologically and ontologically *legitimated* by Enlightenment scientific discourse, it was politically *animated* by a moral vision about the truly just society.

4. See my *States of Injury: Power and Freedom in Late Modernity* (Princeton: Princeton University Press, 1995), chaps. 1–3.

5. The citation from W. Boyd Carpenter is extracted from *The Permanent Elements of Religion: Eight Lectures Preached before the University of Oxford in the Year 1887* (London: Macmillan, 1889), p. 211. Boyd continues on p. 212: "Thus, where inward sympathy with good is lacking, though there may be outward moralism, there can be no true morality."

6. I draw these general characterizations of Machiavelli's and Nietzsche's thought from Machiavelli's *Prince* and *Discourses on Livy* and from Nietzsche's *On the Genealogy of Morals*.

7. Friedrich Nietzsche, *On the Genealogy of Morals*, trans. Walter Kaufmann and R. J. Hollingdale (New York: Vintage, 1969).

8. Niccolò Machiavelli, *The Prince*, chap. 18, in *The Chief Works and Others*, trans. Allan Gilbert (Durham, N.C.: Duke University Press, 1965), 1:66.

9. Ibid.

10. Nietzsche, *On the Genealogy of Morals*, p. 87.

11. One might use this distinction between the moralistic and moral to read various attempts to render the figure of Rodney King in a discourse of martyrdom. Unquestionably an icon of late-twentieth-century racist police violence, in terms of what imaginary struggle or radically transformed future could this King be drawn as a martyr rather than a mere victim?

12. Stuart Hall makes a similar point: "We find it easier to be righteously moralistic about Thatcherism ('isn't she a cow?'): harder to grasp its logic as a political strategy. . . . Our sectarianism is often a product of fear—the changing world is seen as a strange and threatening place without signposts. It is also symptomatic of the way our [left] thinking has become stuck in a particular historic groove" (*The Hard Road to Renewal*, p. 273).

13. The talk from which these remarks are excerpted has now been published as a longer essay titled "The Impossibility of Women's Studies" in a special issue of *Differences* (9, no. 3 [1997]: 79–101) on the future of women's studies, edited by Joan Wallach Scott.

14. Henry Louis Gates, Jr., "Truth or Consequences: Putting Limits on Limits," in *The Limits of Power in American Intellectual Life*, American Council of Learned Societies Occasional Paper No. 22 (New York: American Council of Learned Societies, 1993), p. 19.

15. For an insightful discussion of this intellectual fundamentalism, see William Connolly's *Ethos of Pluralization* (Minneapolis: University of Minnesota Press, 1995), especially chap. 1.

16. William Connolly has articulated this claim regarding the contestable in intellectual morality in much of his recent work. See especially *The Ethos of Pluralization* and *Why I Am Not a Secularist* (Minneapolis: University of Minnesota Press, 1999).

17. Richard Rorty, *Achieving Our Country: Leftist Thought in Twentieth-Century America* (Cambridge, Mass.: Harvard University Press, 1998).

18. Stuart Hall, "Identity in Question," a public lecture at the University of California, Santa Cruz, March 21, 1991.

19. Benedetto Croce, *Politics and Morals*, trans. Salvatore J. Castiglione (London: Allen and Unwin, 1946), p. 43.

20. Michel Foucault, "The Concern for Truth," interview by François Ewald, trans. Alan Sheridan, in *Politics, Philosophy, Culture: Interviews and Other Writings, 1977–1984*, ed. Lawrence D. Kritzman (New York: Routledge, 1988), p. 263.

21. Maurice Merleau-Ponty, "Sartre, Merleau-Ponty: Les lettres d'une rupture," *Magazine Littéraire*, no. 320 (April 1994): 74–76. Thanks to Ivan Ascher for a precise translation.

CHAPTER THREE
THE DESIRE TO BE PUNISHED:
FREUD'S "'A CHILD IS
BEING BEATEN'"

1. Friedrich Nietzsche, *On the Genealogy of Morals*, trans. Walter Kaufmann and R. J. Hollingdale (New York: Vintage, 1969), p. 72.

2. For a discussion of citizenship as the project of making democracy, rather than simply inhabiting it, see Sheldon Wolin, "Constitutional Order, Revolutionary Violence and Modern Power: An Essay of Juxtapositions," an occasional paper published by the Department of Political Science, York University, Toronto, 1990.

3. For a Freudian and Foucaultian consideration of the problem of subjectivization and the problem of desiring freedom, see Judith Butler, *The Psychic Life of Power: Theories in Subjection* (Stanford: Stanford University Press, 1997).

4. Sigmund Freud, " 'A Child Is Being Beaten': A Contribution to the Study of the Origin of Sexual Perversions," trans. Alix and James Strachey, in *Sexuality and the Psychology of Love*, ed. Philip Rieff (New York: Collier Books, 1963), p. 132. This work is hereafter cited parenthetically in the text.

5. Dorothy Allison's work of contemporary fiction *Bastard out of Carolina* (New York: Plume/Penguin, 1992), as well as her autobiographical meditation *Two or Three Things I Know for Sure* (New York: Dutton, 1995), suggests that this phase is indeed sometimes remembered.

6. For the reasons given, I have concentrated my attention on " 'A Child Is Being Beaten' " rather than on other writings on masochism (by Freud or others), including "The Economic Problem in Masochism" and "Instincts and Their Vicissitudes" by Freud (in vols. 19 and 14, respectively, of *The Standard Edition of the Complete Psychological Works of Sigmund Freud*, trans. and ed. James Strachey [London: Hogarth Press, 1974]), "Coldness and Cruelty" by Gilles Deleuze (in *Masochism: Coldness and Cruelty*, by Gilles Deleuze et al., trans. Jean McNeil [New York: Zone Books, 1991]), and ruminations on the subject by Leo Bersani in various texts. Deleuze's work, for example, rehabilitates the literary and psychological contours of the work of Sacher-Masoch, with the ultimate aim of sharply distinguishing masochistic desire and identity from that of sadism, presented here not as mirrors of one another but as profoundly different character formations. Certainly there is nothing amiss about this effort; but unlike " 'A Child Is Being Beaten,' " it does not help us understand the vacillations in punitive desire shaped by early attachments.

7. In Mari Matsuda et al., *Words That Wound: Critical Race Theory, Assaultive Speech, and the First Amendment* (Boulder, Colo.: Westview Press, 1993),

see especially the opening of chaps. 2 and 3. In Catharine A. MacKinnon, *Only Words* (Cambridge, Mass.: Harvard University Press, 1993), see the opening paragraphs of chap. 1.

8. Nietzsche, *On the Genealogy of Morals*, p. 127.

CHAPTER FOUR
POWER WITHOUT LOGIC
WITHOUT MARX

1. Karl Marx, *The German Ideology*, in *The Marx-Engels Reader*, ed. Robert C. Tucker, 2nd ed. (New York: Norton, 1978), pp. 161–62.

2. Etienne Balibar continues: "He was to build the most powerful and comprehensive 'heteronomic' theory of politics in the history of philosophy, which relies on a provocative 'materialist' identification of politics with its 'other': what I call a *short circuit* of 'politics' and 'economy,' arising from the simultaneous economic critique of 'politicism' and political critique of 'economism.' " *Masses, Classes, Ideas: Studies on Politics and Philosophy Before and After Marx*, trans. James Swenson (New York: Routledge, 1994), p. xi.

3. Karl Marx, "Society and Economy in History," in *The Marx-Engels Reader*, pp. 136–37.

4. Marx, *German Ideology*, p. 163.

5. In what follows, I will be moving between the "early" and "late" Marx with impunity, notwithstanding his writings' changes of emphasis regarding power's shape and location.

6. Karl Marx, *Capital*, trans. Samuel Moore and Edward Aveling, ed. Frederick Engels, 3 vols. (New York: International Publishers, 1967), 1:176.

7. Ibid., 3:817.

8. Ibid.

9. Ibid., 1:176, emphasis added.

10. Ibid., 3:827.

11. Karl Marx and Friedrich Engels, "Manifesto of the Communist Party," in *The Marx-Engels Reader*, p. 474.

12. Marx, *German Ideology*, p. 164.

13. Of course, Plato too recognized this attribute of power, but justified depriving everyone of it by pointing to the beneficence of the philosophers at the helm. Plato differs from Marx as well in his appreciation of power's permanence in a polity—hence his solution, to place it in the hands of those presumably uninterested in exploiting or even having it.

14. Marx, *Capital*, 3:819.

15. Marx's famous discussion of freedom and necessity in volume 3 of *Capital* is instructive here:

Just as the savage must wrestle with Nature to satisfy his wants, to maintain and reproduce life, so must civilised man, and he must do so in all social formations and under all possible modes of production. With this development, this realm of physical necessity expands as a result of his wants; but, at the same time, the forces of production which satisfy these wants also increase. Freedom in this field can only consist in socialised man, the associated producers, rationally regulating their interchange with Nature, bringing it under their common control. . . . But it nonetheless still remains a realm of necessity. Beyond it begins that development of human energy which is an end in itself, the true realm of freedom, which, however, can blossom forth only with this realm of necessity as its basis. (p. 820)

16. Ibid., p. 814.

17. Ibid., 1:233.

18. Karl Marx, *Economic and Philosophic Manuscripts of 1844*, in *The Marx-Engels Reader*, p. 73.

19. Ibid., p. 74.

20. Marx, *German Ideology*, p. 150.

21. The one place that this complexity of the relationship between psyche and economy is probed in experimental fashion is in Marx's critique of Hegel's *Phenomenology* in the *Economic and Philosophic Manuscripts*.

22. Michel Foucault, "Two Lectures," trans. Alessandro Fontana and Pasquale Pasquino, in *Power/Knowledge: Selected Interviews and Other Writings, 1972–1977*, ed. Colin Gordon (New York: Pantheon, 1980).

23. Marx, *Capital*, 1:72.

24. What is the significance of this misreading on Foucault's part? That is, what does it mean that Foucault's reading of Marx on power engages in the very mystification that Marx criticizes in his theory of power?

25. Marx, *Capital*, 1:72, emphasis added.

26. Ibid.

27. Foucault, "Two Lectures," p. 88.

28. Marx, *Capital*, 1:80.

29. In *The Philosophy of Marx*, trans. Chris Turner (London: Verso, 1995), Etienne Balibar suggests that Marx *replaced* the notion of ideology with the concept of fetishism. Fetishism does not, in Balibar's view, "represent a mere terminological variant [on ideology], but a genuine theoretical alternative, which has undeniable philosophical implications" (p. 42). With due appreciation for the interesting analysis following this claim, I want to argue for more continuity between the two notions than does Balibar.

30. Marx, *German Ideology*, p. 154.

31. Marx, *Capital*, 1:79.

32. Marx, *German Ideology*, p. 154, emphases added. This work is hereafter cited parenthetically in the text.

NOTES TO CHAPTER 5 · 181

33. Marx, *Capital*, 1:80.

34. As Marx puts the matter in reverse, "this consolidation of what we our-selves produce into an objective power above us, growing out of our control, thwarting our expectations, bringing to naught our calculations, is one of the chief factor in historical development up till now" (*German Ideology*, p. 160).

35. Karl Marx, "On the Jewish Question," in *The Marx-Engels Reader*, p. 33.

36. Marx, *Economic and Philosophic Manuscripts of 1844*, pp. 74–78.

37. Marx, "Jewish Question," p. 34.

38. Ibid., p. 35.

39. Louis Althusser, *For Marx*, trans. Ben Brewster (London: Allen Lane, 1969), pp. 233–34.

40. Marx, "Jewish Question," pp. 35, 46.

41. Ibid., p. 32.

42. See Louis Althusser, "Ideology and Ideological State Apparatuses (Notes towards an Investigation)," in *Lenin and Philosophy and Other Essays*, trans. Ben Brewster (London: New Left Books, 1971).

43. Marx, "Jewish Question," pp. 45–46.

44. Marx, *German Ideology*, p. 163.

45. Marx, *Capital*, 1:72.

46. Marx, "Jewish Question," p. 32.

CHAPTER FIVE
POLITICS WITHOUT BANISTERS:
GENEALOGICAL POLITICS IN
NIETZSCHE AND FOUCAULT

1. Alison Mitchell, "Now, It's the Rhetorical Presidency," *New York Times*, March 31, 1996, sec. 4, pp. 1, 3.

2. Max Weber, "Politics as a Vocation," in *From Max Weber: Essays in Sociol-ogy*, trans. H. H. Gerth and C. Wright Mills (New York: Oxford University Press, 1946), pp. 120–26.

3. Friedrich Nietzsche, *On the Genealogy of Morals*, trans. Walter Kaufmann and R. J. Hollingdale (New York: Vintage, 1969), p. 15. This work is hereafter cited parenthetically in the text.

4. Michel Foucault, "Nietzsche, Genealogy, History," trans. Donald F. Bou-chard and Sherry Simon, in *The Foucault Reader*, ed. Paul Rabinow (New York: Pantheon, 1984), p. 80. This work is hereafter cited parenthetically in the text.

5. Michel Foucault, "Prison Talk," trans. Colin Gordon, in *Power/Knowledge: Selected Interviews and Other Writings, 1972–1977*, ed. Colin Gordon (New York: Pantheon, 1980), p. 50.

6. Michel Foucault, "The Art of Telling the Truth," trans. Jeremy Harding, in *Politics, Philosophy, Culture: Interviews and Other Writings, 1977–1984*, ed. Lawrence D. Kritzman (New York: Routledge, 1988), pp. 87, 95.

7. Michel Foucault, "Critical Theory/Intellectual History," trans. Jeremy Harding, p. 36, and "The Art of Telling the Truth," p. 95, both in *Politics, Philosophy, Culture*.

8. In "What Is Enlightenment?" Kant writes, "If we are asked 'Do we now live in an *enlightened age*?' the answer is 'No,' but we do live in an *age of enlightenment*. As things now stand, much is lacking which prevents men from being, or easily becoming, capable of correctly using their own reason in religious matters with assurance and free from outside direction. But, on the other hand, we have clear indications that the field has now been opened where men may freely deal with these things." *Foundations of the Metaphysics of Morals*, trans. Lewis White Beck, 2nd ed. (New York: Macmillan/Library of Liberal Arts, 1990), p. 88.

9. Foucault, "Critical Theory/Intellectual History," p. 36.

10. Michel Foucault, "Politics and Reason," in *Politics, Philosophy, Culture*, p. 71.

11. Colin Gordon, "Governmental Rationality: An Introduction," in *The Foucault Effect: Studies in Governmentality*, ed. Graham Burchell, Colin Gordon, and Peter Miller (Chicago: University of Chicago Press, 1991), p. 10.

12. Michel Foucault, "Politics and Ethics: An Interview," interview by Paul Rabinow, Charles Taylor, Martin Jay, Richard Rorty, and Leo Lowenthal, trans. Catherine Porter, in *The Foucault Reader*, p. 375.

13. Foucault, "Politics and Reason," pp. 77–79.

14. Gordon, "Governmental Rationality," p. 10.

15. Ibid.

16. Foucault, "Politics and Reason," p. 77.

17. Ibid., p. 79.

18. Foucault, "Nietzsche, Genealogy, History," p. 88.

19. Ibid., p. 89.

20. Foucault, "Critical Theory/Intellectual History," p. 36.

21. Michel Foucault, "Polemics, Politics, and Problematizations," trans. Lydia Davis, in *The Foucault Reader*, p. 381.

22. Michel Foucault, "Truth and Power," in *Power/Knowledge*, p. 133, emphasis added. For his general argument on behalf of the "local" or "specific" intellectual, see pp. 126–33.

23. Foucault, "Politics and Reason," p. 84.

24. Ibid., pp. 59, 84.

25. Ibid., p. 85.

26. Ibid., p. 60.

27. Ibid., pp. 60, 84.

28. Ibid., pp. 84–85.

29. Ibid., p. 83.

30. On Foucault's effort to spatialize power, see, of course, *Discipline and Punish: The Birth of the Prison*, trans. Alan Sheridan (New York: Pantheon, 1977); but see also "Questions on Geography," pp. 69–71, and "The Eye of Power," pp. 149–51, both in *Power/Knowledge*.

31. Foucault, "Questions on Geography," p. 69.

32. Ibid., pp. 70–71.

33. Foucault, "Critical Theory/Intellectual History," p. 37.

34. In *On the Genealogy of Morals*, Nietzsche writes, "[T]he cause of the origin of a thing and its eventual utility, its actual employment and place in a system of purposes, lie worlds apart; whatever exists, having somehow come into being, is again and again reinterpreted to new ends, taken over, transformed, and redirected" (p. 77).

CHAPTER SIX
DEMOCRACY AGAINST ITSELF:
NIETZSCHE'S CHALLENGE

1. The autonomy of both the political and the theoretical domains has been eroded by a range of forces—politics by bureaucracy, political economy, technology, mass media, and privatized functions of the state, and theory by a variety of other interpretive practices including ethnography, all manner of social science, journalism, and most recently literary criticism. Thus, even as the relationship between theory and politics has been stabilized by certain modernist conventions, each individually has grown uncertain and insecure.

2. And frequently, political ideology is thought to be derivable from political biography. For an instance of recent analysis that engages in this conflation, see Lutz Niethammer, *Posthistoire: Has History Come to an End?* trans. Patrick Camiller (London: Verso, 1992), chap. 7.

3. Stuart Hall, "Identity in Question," a public lecture at the University of California, Santa Cruz, March 21, 1991.

4. In Michel Foucault's phraseology, "power is tolerable only on condition that it mask a substantial part of itself. Its success is proportional to its ability to hide its own mechanisms." *The History of Sexuality*, vol. 1, *An Introduction*, trans. Robert Hurley (New York: Vintage, 1978), p. 86.

5. Alexis de Tocqueville, *Democracy in America*, trans. George Lawrence, ed. J. P. Mayer and Max Lerner, 2 vols. in 1 (New York: Harper and Row, 1966), 2:435.

6. Etienne Balibar, "Spinoza, the Anti-Orwell," in *Masses, Classes, Ideas: Studies in Philosophy Before and After Marx*, trans. James Swenson (New York: Routledge, 1994), pp. 24, 25.

7. Benedict de Spinoza, *The Political Works*, ed. and trans. A. G. Wernham (Oxford: Clarendon, 1958).

8. Balibar, "Spinoza, the Anti-Orwell," p. 26.

9. Tocqueville, *Democracy in America*, 2:433–34.

10. Ibid., 2:692–93.

11. Tracy Strong, *Friedrich Nietzsche and the Politics of Transfiguration* (Berkeley: University of California Press, 1975); Richard Rorty, *Philosophy and the Mirror of Nature* (Princeton: Princeton University Press, 1979); Bonnie Honig, *Political Theory and the Displacement of Politics* (Ithaca, N.Y.: Cornell University Press, 1993); William Connolly, *Identity/Difference: Democratic Negotiations of Political Paradox* (Ithaca, N.Y.: Cornell University Press, 1991), *The Ethos of Pluralization* (Minneapolis: University of Minnesota Press, 1995), and *Why I Am Not a Secularist* (Minneapolis: University of Minnesota Press, 1999); Michel Foucault, "Critical Theory/Intellectual History," trans. Jeremy Harding, in *Politics, Philosophy, Culture: Interviews and Other Writings, 1977–1984*, ed. Lawrence D. Kritzman (New York: Routledge, 1988).

12. Friedrich Nietzsche, *On the Genealogy of Morals*, trans. Walter Kaufmann and R. J. Hollingdale (New York: Vintage, 1969), p. 15.

13. Niccolò Machiavelli, *Discourses on the First Decade of Titus Livius*, book 3, chapter 1, in *The Chief Works and Others*, trans. Allan Gilbert (Durham, N.C.: Duke University Press, 1965), 3:419.

14. Friedrich Nietzsche, *Twilight of the Idols*, trans. R. J. Hollingdale (New York: Penguin, 1968), p. 29. This work is hereafter cited parenthetically in the text.

15. In *Twilight of the Idols*, this disdain is expressed as "liberalism: in plain words, *reduction to the herd animal*" (p. 92). In *Thus Spoke Zarathustra*, it is captured in the parable "On the Flies of the Marketplace" (First Part, chapter 12); see *The Portable Nietzsche*, ed. and trans. Walter Kaufmann (New York: Viking, 1954).

16. Nietzsche, *Thus Spoke Zarathustra*, p. 213.

17. Ibid., pp. 160, 162.

18. Friedrich Nietzsche, "Notes" (1875), in *The Portable Nietzsche*, p. 50.

19. Friedrich Nietzsche, *The Will to Power*, in *The Complete Works of Friedrich Nietzsche*, ed. Oscar Levy, vol. 15 (Edinburgh: T. N. Foulis, 1913), p. 205.

20. Nietzsche, *Will to Power*, pp. 184, 227.

21. Friedrich Nietzsche, *Human, All Too Human: A Book for Free Spirits*, trans. Marion Faber with Stephen Lehmann (Lincoln: University of Nebraska Press, 1984), p. 246.

22. Nietzsche, *Twilight of the Idols*, pp. 108–10.

23. Nietzsche, *Human, All Too Human*, p. 230.

24. Ibid., p. 227.

25. See Sheldon Wolin, "Fugitive Democracy," in *Democracy and Difference: Contesting the Boundaries of the Political*, ed. Seyla Benhabib (Princeton: Princeton University Press, 1996).

26. Nietzsche, *Human, All Too Human*, p. 221. It is difficult not to think here of the campaign for gay and lesbian marriage, in which a potentially insurgent practice of love and sexuality seeks housing in an institution that itself is organized to prohibit such insurgency.

27. Nietzsche, *Twilight of the Idols*, p. 23.

28. Nietzsche, *On the Genealogy of Morals*, p. 11.

29. "No *one* is accountable for existing at all, or for being constituted as he is. . . . We invented the concept 'purpose': in reality purpose is *lacking*. . . . We deny God; in denying God, we deny accountability: only by doing *that* do we redeem the world" (Nietzsche, *Twilight of the Idols*, p. 54).

30. Nietzsche, *Thus Spoke Zarathustra*, p. 168.

31. Ibid., p. 137.

32. Political thinkers as diverse as Rousseau, Arendt, Foucault, and Wolin contribute to this perspective on how institutionalization affects democracy.

33. For a consideration of this antidemocratic bind and the possibility of a democratic response to it that focuses on constitutionalism rather than on the state, see Sheldon Wolin's "Constitutional Order, Revolutionary Violence, and Modern Power: An Essay of Juxtapositions," an occasional paper published by the Department of Political Science, York University, Ontario, 1990, and "Fugitive Democracy."

CHAPTER SEVEN
SPECTERS AND ANGELS:
BENJAMIN AND DERRIDA

1. See Elisabeth Young-Bruehl, *Hannah Arendt: For Love of the World* (New Haven: Yale University Press, 1982).

2. Sheldon Wolin, "Political Theory: From Vocation to Invocation," in *Vocations of Political Theory*, ed. Jason Frank and John Tambornino (Minneapolis: University of Minnesota Press, 2000), p. 5.

3. Michael P. Steinberg, introduction to *Walter Benjamin and the Demands of History*, ed. Michael P. Steinberg (Ithaca, N.Y.: Cornell University Press, 1996), p. 15.

4. Jacques Derrida, *Specters of Marx: The State of the Debt, and the Work of Mourning, and the New International*, trans. Peggy Kamuf (New York: Routledge, 1994), p. xvii. This work is hereafter cited parenthetically in the text.

5. Derrida's meditation on justice in "Force of Law: The 'Mystical Foundation of Authority,' " which includes a close deconstructive reading of Benjamin, has a rather different (although not obviously incompatible) set of emphases from those in *Specters of Marx*. See *Cardozo Law Review* 11 (1990): 919–1045.

6. Karl Marx and Friedrich Engels, "The Manifesto of the Communist Party," in *The Marx-Engels Reader*, ed. Robert C. Tucker, 2nd ed. (New York: Norton, 1978), p. 473.

7. Mark Poster's analysis of *Specters of Marx* emphasizes strongly Derrida's (and deconstruction's) claim to be Marx's proper heir: "Derrida boldly proposes to improve upon Marx, to eliminate his 'pre-deconstructive' limitation, to 'radicalize' him, and calls for 'a new International' that will instantiate 'a new Enlightenment for the century to come.' " "Textual Agents: History at 'The End of History,' " in *"Culture" and the Problem of the Disciplines*, ed. John Carlos Rowe (New York: Columbia University Press, 1998), p. 217.

8. Irving Wohlfarth argues that "actuality is, *pace* Nietzsche, the eternal return of what is *not* the same." "The Measure of the Possible, the Weight of the Real, and the Heat of the Moment: Benjamin's Actuality Today," *New Formations*, special issue titled "The Actuality of Walter Benjamin," no. 20 (summer 1993): 4.

9. Walter Benjamin, "Theses on the Philosophy of History," in *Illuminations*, ed. Hannah Arendt, trans. Harry Zohn (New York: Schocken, 1969), p. 257. This work is hereafter cited parenthetically in the text.

10. Lutz Niethammer, *Posthistoire: Has History Come to an End?* trans. Patrick Camiller (London: Verso, 1992), pp. 119–20.

11. Walter Benjamin, "N: [Re The Theory of Knowledge, Theory of Progress]" (an excerpt from *The Arcades Project*), in *Benjamin: Philosophy, History, Aesthetics*, ed. Gary Smith (Chicago: University of Chicago Press, 1989), p. 55.

12. Benjamin's critique is often (mis)read through Theodor Adorno's rejoinder to it in "Progress," in Smith, *Benjamin*.

13. Gershom Scholem, "Walter Benjamin and His Angel," in *On Walter Benjamin: Critical Essays and Recollections*, ed. Gary Smith (Cambridge, Mass.: MIT Press, 1988), p. 65.

14. Ibid., p. 83.

15. Niethammer, *Posthistoire*, p. 111.

16. Ibid.

17. Marx makes a similar point about the character of progress in his claim that "each new class which puts itself in the place of one ruling before it, is compelled . . . to represent its interest as the common interest of all the members of society[;] . . . it has to give its ideas the form of universality and represent them as the only rational, universally valid ones." *The German Ideology*, in *The Marx-Engels Reader*, p. 174.

18. Benjamin, "N," pp. 65, 66.

19. Wohlfarth, "The Measure of the Possible," pp. 2, 4.

20. Ibid., pp. 5, 2.

21. Benjamin, "N," p. 49.

22. Ibid., p. 67.

23. Ibid., p. 61.

24. Ibid., p. 51.

25. Ibid., pp. 60, 64.

26. The longer passage from which this phrase is drawn is instructive: "We know that the Jews were prohibited from investigating the future. The Torah and the prayers instruct them in remembrance, however. This stripped the future of its magic, to which all those succumb who turn to the soothsayers for enlightenment. This does not imply, however, that for the Jews the future turned into homogenous, empty time. For every second of time was the strait gate through which the Messiah might enter" ("Theses on the Philosophy of History," p. 264).

27. For Benjamin's bewitching formulation of the "Then" and the "Now" as political terms unapproachable by "Past" and "Present," see "N," especially pp. 49, 51–52, 80.

28. Wohlfarth, "The Measure of the Possible," p. 2.

29. Sigmund Freud, "Mourning and Melancholia," in The Standard Edition of the Complete Psychological Works, ed. and trans. James Strachey, vol. 14 (London: Hogarth, 1957), p. 245.

30. Ibid. This sharp distinction between melancholia and mourning may be something of an overstatement on Freud's part. Surely mourning includes unconscious dimensions of loss and attachment, just as it often triggers a chain of unconscious losses that are only indirectly related to the overtly lost object.

31. Walter Benjamin, The Origin of German Tragic Drama, trans. John Osborne (London: Verso, 1977), pp. 156–57.

32. Walter Benjamin, "Left Wing Melancholy," trans. Ben Brewster, in The Weimar Republic Sourcebook, ed. Anton Kaes, Martin Jay, and Edward Dimendberg (Berkeley: University of California Press, 1994), p. 305.

33. Wohlfarth, "The Measure of the Possible," p. 3.

34. Benjamin, "N," p. 55.

35. Norbert Bolz and Willem van Reijen, Walter Benjamin, trans. Laimdota Mazzarins (Atlantic Highlands, N.J.: Humanities Press, 1991), p. 19.

INDEX

hate speech, 57
Hegel, 6, 83, 79, 107; dialectic of, 65; *Phenomenology of Mind*, 180n.21
Hill, Anita, 54
historiography, 5, 100–102
history, end of, 6, 16; in Marx, 63–64, and philosophy, 107. *See also* consciousness, historical; historiography
History of Sexuality (Foucault), 96, 183n.4
Hobbes, Thomas, 47
Holocaust, 140–41
Horkheimer, Max, 166
Human, All Too Human (Nietzsche), 91
humanism, 26

Idealism, 82–83, 90
identity: as abstraction, 10, 49, 57; dissolution of, 128–29; disrupted by genealogy, 102; formation of, 58–59; injury and, 38, 54; institutionalization of, 31–34; masochism and, 15, 46; political, 147, 169; politics of, 9, 14, 19, 26, 36–40, 46, 52–57, 110
ideology, 79–81, 87
intellectual, specific vs. universal, 113
interests, 10, 38–39, 43, 79, 84, 99

Jackson, Michael, 60
Jews, 141, 187n.26
judgment, 29, 42
justice, 3, 9, 14, 145–55

Kant, Immanuel, 3, 6, 107, 182n.8; *Foundations of the Metaphysics of Morals*, 182n.8; "What Is Enlightenment?" 107, 182n.8
Kastner, Eric, 170
King, Martin Luther, Jr., 24
King, Rodney, 54, 177n.11
Klee, Paul, "Angelus Novus," 138, 158
Kraus, Karl, 159
Krushchev, Nikolai, 18

labor: commodification of, 72; division of, 80–83; theory of value of, 71
Left, the, 6, 12, 18–19, 21, 168–69

Lerner, Michael, 91
liberalism, 7–9, 13, 20–21, 52; changes in, 9; contemporary, 136; doctrines of, 5–6, 9, 11, 28, 30, 83; historical, 19; institutions of, 39; legitimacy of, 10, 14; *post-histoire*, 3
Locke, John, 47
Lovelace, Linda, 53

Machiavelli, 7, 24, 27, 118, 128
MacKinnon, Catherine, 53–54; *Only Words*, 54
Maoism, 110
Marcuse, Herbert, 19, 47
marriage, gay and lesbian, 36, 185n.26
Marx, Karl, 6, 47, 62–90, 142, 144, 148, 151, 154–56, 165, 167, 171, 179n.13, 179n.15, 181n.34, 186n.7, 186n.17; *camera obscura* in, 66, 77; *Capital*, 70, 77–78, 89; on capital, 70; on civil society, 65; "Communist Manifesto," 148–49; "Critique of Hegel's Philosophy of Right," 84; critique of Hegel, 83, 180n.21; *Economic and Philosophic Manuscripts of 1844*, 151, 180n.21; *The German Ideology*, 75, 77, 79, 186n.17; on ideology, 79–81, 87; "On the Jewish Question," 77, 84, 85 87; on power, 16, 62–82, 89–90; production in, 67–68; scientism of, 16, 65–67, 70–73, 79; and the state, 84–88
Marxism, 11, 19, 110, 144, 161, 165–66, 172–73; on truth, 28; and poststructuralism, 62–63; on power, 62
masochism: and identity, 15, 46, 55, 60–61; and power, 52–53. *See also* Freud
mass, the state and, 123–24
Matsuda, Mari, et al., *Words that Wound*, 54, 176n.3
"Measure of the Possible" (Wolfarth), 138, 186n.7
melancholia, Left, 169. *See also* Benjamin, Walter
melancholy, 4, 44; vs. mourning, 187n.30
memory, 150, 168

ressentiment, 129–30, 132
Right, the, 6, 12, 19, 21, 38
rights, 9, 11, 12, 14, 35
Rorty, Richard, 40
Rousseau, Jean-Jacques, 131, 175n.3, 185n.32, as a critic of modernity, 7
Russia, 7

Saint Paul, 92
Sartre, Jean-Paul, 43
scientism, in Marx, 16, 65–67, 70–73, 79
sexuality, 20, 36, 52, 141
Shakespeare, 153–54; Hamlet, 153; Timon of Athens, 151
Shepard, Matthew, 54
Simpson, O. J., 60
Smith, Adam, 71
social contract, 12
Sophists, 24
sovereignty, 3–4, 11
specters. See ghosts
Specters of Marx (Derrida), 143–55, 185n.5, 186n.7
speech codes, 35–36
Spinoza, Benedict de, 123–24, 128, 136; Tractatus Politicus, 124
Stalin, Joseph, 19
state, 11, 13, 36, 83, 85; as fetish, 88–89; Marx's critique of, 83; welfare, 6, 8, 13
subject, 10, 15, 22, 38; formation of, 46; in Foucault, 47, 99; as sovereign, 11, 30

Techniques of the Self (Foucault), 42–43
teleology, 5, 16, 148

theory, political, 3, 29, 121–24, 133–35; and politics, 41, 122–26, 133–35
Thucydides, 7, 24
Thus Spoke Zarathustra (Nietzsche), 121, 134
Timon of Athens (Shakespeare), 151
Tocqueville, Alexis de, 6, 123–26, 136
tolerance, 131
Trauerspiel (Benjamin), 170
Tractatus Politicus (Spinoza), 124
Truman, Harry, 7
Twilight of the Idols (Nietzsche), 121, 129, 131
Tyson, Michael, 60

universalism, 9, 27–28
Use of Pleasure (Foucault), 42–43

Vico, Giambattista, 7
victimization, 53–55
Vidal, Gore, 6–7
violence: fantasies of, 46–61; vs. governmental rationality, 114

Weber, Max, 35, 47, 92–93
Wolfarth, Irving, 164; "The Measure of the Possible," 138, 186n.7
Wolin, Sheldon, 142, 185n.32, 185n.33; "Constitutional Order, Revolutionary Violence," 185n.33
women, 28, 55. See also gender
Words that Wound (Matsuda et al.), 54, 176n.3

Yeats, William Butler, 92
Yugoslavia, 7